To my grandchildren, Max and Lucy-May,

because I'm missing you.

Yards and Fences, Gates and Roads

or . . . what Grandma did when she was a little girl

Written and illustrated by Carol Sullivan Johnson

From the author

Dear Reader,

When I began this whimsical excursion down memory lane, it was in response to a recurring dream about an old lichen-covered fence. In the weeks it has taken to bring this book to publication, our world has changed beyond anything I could have imagined.

While my thoughts have been occupied with the past, in the present, nations all over the world have been plunged into a trauma of disease and death which will undoubtedly change the way we will all live our lives in the future. I hope, when this crisis has passed, that we can and will rebuild a kinder and more cohesive world.

For those who have lost loved ones at this time, may you find solace and come to a place of peace.

So many memories from my childhood have surfaced during the writing of this book that I could not include them all. I have barely mentioned wider family or friends, and for that, I apologise.

I hope that these light-hearted stories will bring each reader a great deal of pleasure while also helping to preserve a sense of the historic Mt Gravatt in which I grew up.

Carol Sullivan Johnson

7th April 2020, Halstead, UK.

Contents

Chapter 1 7

Fences 7

Chapter 2 24

Up our Hill 24

Chapter 3 46

Traffic 46

Chapter 4 59

Fruits and Flowers 59

Chapter 5 71

Bugs 71

Chapter 6 86

Reptiles, Birds and Furry Things 86

Chapter 7 101

Our House 101

Chapter 8 128

The Creek 128

Chapter 9 148

An Old New World 148

Maps 155

Pictures 160

Addendum 167

Chapter 1

Fences

They say that at the point of death, your whole life flashes before your eyes. Funnily enough, the same can be said for having to spend days and weeks in enforced isolation due to the pandemic that is currently spreading across our world. Only, unlike the imminent death scenario, in the dreary, grey, end-of-winter days of housebound solitude, my whole life isn't exactly flashing. It's just rolling out, night after night, in forensically-detailed slow motion.

In fact, I suspect, it is those very restrictions themselves which are giving rise to my recurring nocturnal wanderings: vivid dreams about fences. Recollections of every fence I have ever encountered – from the very earliest memories of my own back yard's boundaries, growing up on a post-war housing estate in suburban Brisbane, to the fences and walls of a thousand front yards I have wandered past, leant on or peered over, present themselves to my mind's eye in graphic, technicolour detail. I find myself, basically, fence obsessed.

Not one to ignore a creative urge, or the opportunity to express it, I am using my forced confinement to wander down memory lane and record the stories of my youth that were sufficiently significant to have been retained for almost all of my 60 years. My hope is that by the time our nationwide quarantine has ended, I will have compiled a series of tales of a bygone era that will both amuse and inform my young grandchildren (whose chubby little hands I am longing to hold and whose enthusiastic hugs and kisses are sorely missed), perhaps be enjoyed by other children, and encourage other parents and grandparents to share their own childhood memories.

Each fence marks the personal space of the family units living within.

Each of my dreamtime fences encloses a unique space, a microcosm of suburban life, like individual cells in the great hive of humanity. Each fence marks the personal space of the family units living within, which, I would be taught soon enough, make up the fabric of our community – the basis of society itself.

In Australia, the decade which was the 1960s was a time of social transformation and modernisation. A new national identity was being forged, as the populace began to turn away from the sorrows and deprivation of wars and rumours of wars, and move towards an up-swell of self-discovery and aspiration: the birth pangs of the nation's modern era. They were exciting times, a great world opportunity – I see with hindsight – but my focus, as a child born in 1960, was solely riveted on the comings and goings of the living things that called the area enclosed by our neighbourhood's boundary fences 'home'.

In fact, it was not world events but the geography of the area itself which determined much of the character-forming nature of these 'comings and goings'. It was challenging for the residents of the box-like brick and wooden houses which clung to the sides of the steep streets and lanes of Mt Gravatt's foothills to get about and, as they say: "Necessity is the mother of invention." The common need to move about on foot from point A to point B fostered in the local community a sense of neighbourliness which allowed far more liberal access across barriers than may be tolerated today.

Giving my dream-brain free reign to sift through my farthest memories, I can recall many of the fences which, in my infancy, marked the limits of each of the neighbourhood families' places in the world. I pass from one fence to the next – from my favourite lichen-covered, wooden-paling side fence (which was home to the broadest range of animal life in the whole of the back yard and an Aladdin's cave of hidden treasure which had been dropped between the fence and the neighbour's old asbestos garage) to the deep and impenetrable barrier at the bottom of the garden formed by grass so tall, it had all but devoured the ramshackle fence into which it grew.

According to my mother, this nether region of our yard, which began with a clump of straggly bananas with trunks that sounded hollow when they were tapped, was likely to harbour many of the native beasts which would rapidly put paid to a young life such as mine, should I be unfortunate enough to encounter them. For this reason, the whole area was fastidiously avoided. The only occasion I remember venturing into it out of curiosity (and probably defiance) had me back-tracking in panic when I realised I could no longer see above the tops of the grass stalks.

Although this inhospitable strip of neglected ground may or may not have harboured venomous snakes or spiders, it certainly was home to an eclectic array of scrap, from old, rusty car parts; defunct farming equipment; the odd shoe or rusted pair of scissors; as well as various obsolete enamel household goods. In fact, anything which had come to the end of its useful life was disposed of by 'chucking it down the back'.

The deep and impenetrable barrier at the bottom of the garden.

Nearly every household on our stretch of street had a 'down the back' at some time or other. The grass was left to its own devices, growing tall and sharp, sending up spears of honey-coloured seeds over which sparrows noisily squabbled. Its rustling, serrated blades would shoot for the sky, then die right back to the base, weaving themselves into clumps of matted, brown, fibrous material. This dry grass could be teased out by dextrous fingers and plaited to make wristbands or necklaces, like those worn by 'hula-hula girls'. I suppose the area was not really that much unlike the rubbish pits dug by householders of yesteryear, before the introduction of civic waste disposal services for the disposal of broken and unwanted goods.

Some local householders were known to keep a pet sheep in the yard to help keep the long grass under control, or a goat, or even a small horse. One such pet, a merino lamb, was resident in a house in Invermore Street, which we passed on our way home from school (if we went the 'back' way). This canny sheep quite liked schoolchildren and would bounce enthusiastically to the front fence when it saw that school was out and gaggles of noisy children were passing by. Bleating for attention, it would poke its fuzzy nose through the wire mesh fence for food.

Although the sheep did an excellent job of keeping the grass short on its own side of the fence, it was always keen to sample the grass on the other side as well. We would take turns to pull up whatever blades we could to poke through the wire and into its crunching, grinding teeth, all the while taking care to avoid having our fingers inadvertently nibbled. It was fascinating to be able to study a sheep at such close range, particularly to watch the strange horizontal pupils in its eyes contract and dilate as it raised and lowered its head. Another of our near neighbours kept a baby kangaroo for a while – a 'jocy' – which happily bounded around their quarter-acre plot, nibbling the grass down, being too small to jump the fence.

When it came time, as it inevitably did, for our back fence to be replaced, 'down the back' had to be cleared and all the rubbish removed. This proved such an onerous task that my father decided the grass needed to be burnt down first. He sought the help of our next-door neighbour, Uncle Arthur, who worked at the oil refinery, to provide him with something he could use to encourage controlled burning. Obligingly, Uncle

Arthur came to the back door the next day and handed over a can of liquid from the refinery. "This'll do it," he assured Dad.

The day arrived for the job to be tackled. My two siblings and I stood a little distance away and watched as Dad sprinkled the contents of the can along the fence line and across the offending swathe of grass. "Stand back," he instructed, as he lit a match and tossed it towards the last place the drops of fuel had fallen.

"Whoosh!" Before the match had even reached it, the patch of dry grass exploded into flames which shot ten feet[1] into the air with an almighty, thundering boom! My sister, Dianne, and my brother Greg, both older than myself, squealed with excitement and delight. I jumped out of my skin. Dad shouted a lot of swear words and ran for the hosepipe.

The patch of dry grass exploded into flames.

Later in the evening, the conflagration having been thoroughly extinguished, my father went next door to ask what had been in the can. Back came the answer. Wanting to be helpful, Uncle

---

[1] Ten feet is approximately three metres.

Arthur had supplied our unwitting dad with a can full of high octane aviation fuel, designed to power jet engines!

In the case of our neighbourhood, it was the generous size of the plots of land[2] (which were actually two narrow plots on which one house was centrally positioned) combined with antiquated manual grass-cutting machinery (push mowers with bladed roller barrels) which ensured that only a minimal amount of space was kept cultivated under low-growing, drought-proof grass – typically, blue-green buffalo grass.

That space would usually incorporate the area to the front of the house, although not necessarily the public footpath; side access for vehicles (possibly) and whatever space was necessary out the back for hanging out clothes on an old gibbet clothesline. The cement path which connected the outside dry toilet (the 'dunny') to the back steps of the house and some access to various fruit trees would also be kept clear. Apart from that, nature was left well alone to take its own course. I used to think that the purpose of the fences in establishing ownership of the ground was not because the space was wanted, but so one neighbour didn't spend time and effort taming another neighbour's wilderness.

With regard to which of our neighbours had the most impressive and dangerous 'down the back', I am spoiled for choice. Our immediate neighbours (and our godparents), Auntie Grace and Uncle Arthur's 'down the back' disappeared abruptly one day when their adjoining neighbour at the bottom

---

[2] Thirty-two perches, in old money, just short of a quarter of an acre (40 perches) which in turn, is about the size of two tennis courts.

of their yard stripped away their shared wooden fence to level his back yard and install an underground swimming pool, which never eventuated. Neither was a retaining wall erected to shore up the exposed face of soil cut out of the sloping ground, so over the years, Auntie Grace's back yard just crumbled down in big clumps of earth, into the neighbour's flat dirt plateau.

On the other side of Auntie Grace's house from us, going uphill, there was a grocery store, 'the shop', about which there is more below. The owners, who were also residents, maintained only a narrow band of grass between the back steps of the shop/house and their outhouse. The remaining bottom half of the yard was entirely given over to nature.

In the middle of it grew an ancient Moreton Bay fig tree, with tiny, round fruits which, when they ripened, were a magnet for dozens of chattering fruit-bats on sticky summer nights. We would sometimes sneak out in the dark and stand in Auntie Grace's back yard, a respectable distance away from the tree, and watch and listen as they flew in and out of the topmost branches in search of the fruit. What a noise they made, and what a stink, as well! If something was tossed into the tree, the flying foxes (as we called them) would all take off at once and their black silhouettes would flash across the midnight blue sky like something from a horror film.

The Moreton Bay fig itself was a good climbing shape with huge buttress roots and it played host to several versions of tree house built with disparate planks of wood from under our house. My brother Greg and other local boys would drag the timber over and, 'borrowing' our father's tools, would bash and saw away, trying to secure the boards in some fashion to the branches so they would form a platform on which to sit and watch the world go by. A lot of boys fell out of that old fig tree.

Because distances were long and climbing the hills so taxing, neighbour allowed neighbour to use the gates in their fences to navigate the streets by the way of least resistance. This was a bonus for customers heading to the shop. The gate in the shop's back fence acted like a funnel for children and adults alike. From several streets away they came in a steady stream, via the property adjoining the rear of the shop, to buy butter, newspapers, tins of beans, or packets of lollies[3].

Through the wooden gate (which swung itself closed with a resounding clump and the reassuring rattle of the iron catch dropping into place) they would come. Nodding their greetings, they would pass each other from different directions on a path through the long grass that ran close to where the side fence of the property would have been, had there still been a side fence there. It had been removed with a promise of replacement by the shop owners. Uncle Arthur did his bit, the top half, the same as his new ranch-style front fence, but the shop was sold shortly after and the new owners, and those after them, didn't quite get around to finishing the job.

Hiking up what had been a side driveway from the back yard of the shop, customers would skirt a raised wall and then turn into the open door at the front. The owners lived on one side of the house, which was arranged in a 'U' shape. A huge display window had been installed into what had originally

---

[3] Lollies are sweets and they could be bought individually, two or three for a penny, and put into small white paper packets. Many a shopkeeper learned patience waiting for a child to choose which lollies they wanted for their thripence.

been the lounge room on the other side of the house to create a small grocery store. Paths in every direction, (on the street or through people's yards) which led to and from the shop, were littered with ice block (ice lolly) wrappers and their wooden sticks, lolly wrappers and empty cigarette cartons. Eventually the shop was sold again, reverted to use as a normal house, and both issues (the fence and the litter) were resolved.

The house that shared the back fence with the shop was owned by a lady called M.E. and sat in the midst of a very impressive block of untended wilderness which joined seamlessly to that behind that shop. If a wildebeest had been looking for a home, it would have been happy at M.E.'s. The property was inhabited by an eccentric woman – the type of character scary stories are written about. Her tumbledown cottage was the haunt of every curious or bored young child in the neighbourhood at some time or other.

M. was about 40 years old, but to my young mind, she seemed much older. She had long, black, wavy hair which she tied up behind her head, except when it had just been washed, when it would hang, loose and thin, almost reaching her waist, and streaked with strands of grey. She lived alone in an old pioneer's shack which sat right at the top of her property, near the grass-choked back fence. It must have been one of the earliest dwellings built in the area.

There were still a few of these rustic brown huts dotted around amongst the post-war houses which had since filled the streets, particularly further out into bushland areas. M.'s consisted of two rooms at the front – a living/dining/kitchen area about 10 feet square,[4] off which came a bedroom of the same dimensions. The front door was entered from a small, covered porch which had a hint of decorative fretwork in the gable. The dozen steps up to the front porch were high and narrow,

[4] Ten feet is about three metres.

but the back door opened out straight onto ground level, so steep was the incline on which the hut had been built.

A lean-to at the back of the kitchen, being slightly larger, served as a general purpose work area with a cement washing trough on the back wall next to the back door. In the corner of the lean-to was a windowless alcove, separated off by corrugated iron walls and a corrugated iron door, which held nothing but a huge, chipped enamel bathtub, a battered washstand, and a naked lightbulb hanging from the timber supporting the iron roof.

Even in broad daylight, it was pitch black in there. The taps for filling the bath passed their pipes through the corrugated iron sheets separating the bathroom from the back of the ancient wood-burning stove in the kitchen on the other side. In turn, the pipes then passed through another hole in the kitchen wall above a sink and out to the water tanks outside.

M. was unusual in many ways, only one of which was that she maintained two water tanks, side by side, one tall and the other squat and fat – the only ones left in the neighbourhood. The hut was so dilapidated, it had been condemned many years prior by the city council as being unfit for human habitation, but M. either couldn't, or wouldn't, do anything about it. When everyone else had town water connected, she continued using her water tanks. She still had her old dry toilet out the back, and I have no idea how it was ever emptied!

M. became my good friend as soon as I realised she was always home and she was always pleased to see me. I would visit her often and rummage through a battered tobacco tin full of trinkets and things such as brooches, badges and plastic dice, or she would just tell me stories about her life. She had been married, but then deserted by her husband, and, regretfully, being childless, spent her days sitting alone in her front room drinking black tea (she had no fridge for milk) sweetened by dipping the tip of a teaspoon into a jar of molasses and then stirring it into the steaming brew. She completed her meal with the thinnest slice possible of plain, white bread, which she cut from a loaf. She was so terribly, terribly poor.

In her bedroom there was a wardrobe and an old iron bed. The walls were undecorated, being just the painted inside of the brown-stained boards outside. The bare dirt under the house was visible through gaps in the floorboards. I only ventured into her bedroom once, when she pulled her wedding gown out of her wardrobe because she wanted to show it to me.

M.'s wedding gown was so elegant, so ornate, I gasped when she laid it out on her bed for me to see. It was made entirely of cream silk guipure lace with a square-necked, fitted bodice and long sleeves which came to a point over the back of the hand. The bodice and skirt were satin lined and hung heavily down to a small train, a loop of fabric being sewn into the back of the skirt to lift the train up off the floor if needed. A line of self-covered buttons ran down the back, and, as was the fashion of its time, the shoulders were squared by heavy padding.

Even at my young age, I could recognise the quality of the lace and the sophistication of the style. I realised at that moment that my friend had been someone else in the past, someone with hope and aspiration for her future. I couldn't squeeze into the gown's tiny, nipped waist and tight fitting bodice, despite being so young.

I was astounded when, perhaps because the topic of our conversation had produced in her a sense of the disappointment and pointlessness of her marriage, she told me I could have the dress to take home with me. I kept its luxurious lace for many years, until, disintegrating and covered in rust spots, it finally made its way to the bin.

Eventually, M. sold her land and moved away. Builders quickly demolished the shabby hut made of iron, rough timber and tar-paper, and tore up the wilderness that surrounded it, including two huge lantana bushes at the front fence – one mauve and one pink and orange. They bulldozed out the broken bits of concrete path and the remains of two rectangular flower beds that flanked the front steps, and dug out a level platform in the wounded earth for sinking foundation trenches. The block was then split lengthways and two long, thin houses erected, much to the satisfaction of the neighbours on all sides.

About the same time that M. sold her property, the shop also stopped trading and reverted back to its original purpose as a residential property. The cut-through across M.'s land was no longer needed, which was probably just as well, as far as the new neighbours in the houses built on her land were

[5]Several years later, as a young teenager trudging down the centre of our street, I encountered M.E. trudging up the other way. My face lit up to see my great friend. She, however, cast her eyes down from mine and, without breaking her stride, passed me by. No doubt she had her reasons, nevertheless, the snub inflicted a painful wound.

concerned. I still used to sneak through their side yard and up to the old gate, which had been left there in the back fence, and take my usual route across Auntie Grace's yard to our side door, but I made sure I was not likely to be seen![5]

The earliest years of my life were mostly restricted to the physical boundaries of the fences of our own property – those now being visited in my dreams. What rich and exotic experiences those years provided! Life for me as a child was so different from that of my children, or my grandchildren, today. While my grandchildren are growing up taking modern technology in their stride, even my children are not old enough to remember a world without instant communication, real-time world news, ready-made meals, or flush toilets. It is not what I didn't have that I remember most about those years of my infancy, but what I did have.

I had such a fascinating array of native flora and fauna inhabiting my little piece of the world that there was always some new and interesting wildlife to encounter and study. For hours, I would watch bugs, utterly engrossed, observing their quirks and curiosities as they went about their business. Entire colonies of these native beetles, lizards and butterflies have now, sadly, risked being almost eradicated, their numbers declining at a speed commensurate with the destruction of their natural habitats and the expansion of residential neighbourhoods.

In the case of mosquitoes (mozzies) this was a welcome development. However, the cost of freedom from the incessant buzzing of those nocturnal mini-vampires was the loss of very many other, beautifully coloured and harmless beetles and moths. Having no pact with the kamikaze mozzie, who liked to strike under cover of darkness, rambunctious armoured beetles of every shape, colour and size would swarm around the kitchen light on sultry summer evenings, bashing and crashing into the bulb, then falling, stunned, down onto the kitchen table beneath. With the clearing of the native bushland[6] to accommodate further house building, the underground channelling of the watercourses, filling of dams and over-building of farmland, the march of civilisation took no heed of the declining wildlife population.

My grandchildren now visit many of these exotic creatures at the zoo, studying them from the other side of a glass wall, but I had the privilege of finding them in the wilds of my own back yard, handling them and studying them at close range. Some, such as the grey, spiny bearded dragons that warmed themselves in the morning sun, camouflaged on the weather-beaten wood of my 'lichen' fence, were captured and trained as pets, for however long I could maintain their captivity. Others were left to their own devices, once my curiosity was satisfied. Some I felt were best left alone altogether – prodded with a stick…maybe.

My back yard was my laboratory. I ate plants I probably shouldn't have eaten. I studied all the flowers with great diligence: bud, flower, stem and leaf, dismembering them with scientific rigour and compiling a mental catalogue of all their parts, and especially their fragrances. Some of the resident caterpillars and beetles could also be induced, with enough poking, to let off a good stink – all of which was duly noted. The spiky ones were carefully avoided.

---

[6] From here on known as 'the bush'

I studied the shades and textures of flowers and leaves, wings, thoraxes and abdomens, legs and tails, until their forms, patterns and habits were indelibly imprinted on my mind. In the two years between my earliest datable memory[7] – the day my brother, Greg, started school – to the day that I started school myself, my yard was my classroom, the natural world was my subject, and self-directed learning was the philosophy of my education.

---

[7] Although I remember playing with my brother beforehand, the day Greg started school is clearly impressed on my mind. It would have been at the end of January, 1964.
Dianne had started school the year before and Mum told me Greg was in the same class that she had started in: Mrs. N.'s class.
Two years later, I, too, would make that long walk up to the school's sweeping front drive, under the big Moreton Bay fig, to join Mrs N.'s class, along with 47 other children. Many of the children I started school with would remain my friends until we graduated from the High School further up the road, twelve years later.

She lived alone in an old pioneer's shack which sat right at the top of her property.

Chapter 2

Up our Hill

After World War II, when houses were sprouting up like mushrooms after rain (thanks in great part to a Mr George Chester), our house, and many others like it, were built on the lower hills east of Mount Gravatt. Nearly every native tree and all the scrubland which had grown in the area had been cleared away to facilitate the building work. Only a few of the largest and most majestic of the gums remained standing. Possibly because they were far enough away from the proposed site of the houses, or possibly because they were too large and difficult to remove, a few of these elegant giants posed with their papery bark robes flowing over silver trunks like marble monuments raised up beside a Roman highway.

One of these lone trees stood on the footpath several doors up the hill from us, outside another little pioneer shack – the residence of a cheerful old lady in her nineties called Mrs G. Mrs G. was a tiny, white-haired lady who walked hunched over a stick and was very nearly blind, but she lived alone in her little brown house two doors up from the shop. The wooden paling fence at the front was very low and the gate hung off it at quite a jaunty angle. The fence was missing several palings and was overgrown with grass and shrubs.

From the open gate, the remains of once neat flower beds ran down each side of what was left of a concrete path. The occasional persistent bloom still poked its face out from amongst the nutgrass by which the beds had been thoroughly choked. The ground around the house hadn't seen a mower for decades and Mrs G.'s back yard was reputedly the habitation of colonies of vicious black wasps whose nests hung undisturbed from some old, ragged, fruit trees. No one knew where the back fence was. But she was a happy and kind, warm-hearted lady who always had a jovial, single-toothed smile of welcome for me when I wandered up the hill to visit her.[8]

The residence of a cheerful old lady in her nineties called Mrs G.

---

[8] All the back doors of the neighbours' houses were left open and I would just walk in and shout, "Yoo-hoo!" to see if anyone was home. They usually were, and I often came away with a biscuit after a nice chat. Once, the lady at the back of ours, Mrs C., gave me a beautiful aurora borealis crystal brooch on one of my visits.

Mrs G.'s little cottage was built of narrow, brown-stained timber boards, tar-paper and corrugated iron, the same as M.E.'s. It also consisted of a couple of rooms, but was a little better appointed and was in slightly better repair than M.'s, which was back to back with Mrs G.'s, but two doors down, facing the opposite way. One of Mrs G.'s front rooms was a sitting room and the other her bedroom. She also had a designated space to use as a kitchen which opened out from the back of the sitting room. It housed a kitchen table and some cupboards, the sink, and I suppose a small bathroom came off that.

On the kitchen wall, a wood-burning stove, as was typical of this type of house, was built into an alcove, and although it opened into the house, it actually protruded from the back wall. The alcove was made of corrugated iron, so as to reduce the risk of the wood-burning stove setting the whole building alight. A ramshackle set of steps went down the back wall to the outhouse.[9]

One particularly nice memory I have of my visits to Mrs G. was that she had sweet and very delicately crocheted lace doilies on her table: a little touch of luxury and elegance in what was otherwise a very Spartan existence. I expect she may have crocheted them herself when her eyes had been good.

When our street had been cleared and laid out, the cars drove to one side of Mrs. G.'s remaining gum tree – the higher side – but the pedestrians took a lower, stony path around it, creating a narrow, wedge-shaped strip of rough grass and tree roots in the middle of the footpath. Amongst these gnarled roots, each year, the cheerful, golden daisy-faces of a lone clump of coreopsis would bob about. I don't know if Mrs G. had

[9] The steps were always the first things to go on these old houses. The resident children would leap out of the open doorways that remained, onto the grass below, to see if they could fly.

planted it there, but it was a wonder it had survived and naturalized.

On the footpath, the remaining gum tree itself was enormous. As its girth increased, it would shed great patches of dark, gnarled bark, exposing a new smooth, silver trunk beneath. Under the bark, the trunk was home to a multitude of insects and the shade afforded by the tree's generous canopy created a cool spot in which travellers could rest after the long, dusty climb up the hill.

As a result of the denuding of the ground in order to build, the occupants of the new houses began to plant their yards with more fashionable, non-native species. Exotic vines and poisonous shrubs from South America, like the goblet of death that is the 'Golden Chalice' and the toxic but elegant 'Angel Trumpet', began to make their appearances. Gourds from Asia (such as the prickly pale green 'choko' which was commonly found draped over outside toilets) and flowers, fruits and vines from other tropical regions, like frangipani and bougainvillea, were very much in vogue. Clouds of mauve jacaranda trumpets of Latin American origin and flaming red boughs of Madagascan poinciana featured in every street.

Many of our flowers came from South Africa as it had a warm, dry climate, similar to South East Queensland's winters. Other species came from more tropical areas, like the islands of the Pacific, because they could tolerate less water, but would flourish in the high heat and humidity of a Brisbane summer. We could also grow citrus fruit and plants from Mediterranean climates, as well as some flowers from temperate climates, such as Northern Europe. Some bulbs grew well, but not those that needed to over-winter in really cold ground, like snowdrops, or daffodils and tulips.

The goblet of death that is the Golden Chalice.

The largely British population of post-war migrants and descendants of early settlers still hankered to grow the perfect rose, planting specimens along their front fences, interspersed with gerberas, zinnia, or drought-resistant succulents from South African soil.

Our godmother, Auntie Grace (a family of 'ten pound Poms' from Blackpool, England, Auntie Grace and Uncle Arthur had arrived in Australia with their two sons in the early 1950s)[10]

10 'Ten pound Poms' were immigrants from Britain who came to Australia after the war on an assisted passage, for which they paid

grew mauve violets whose roots survived in the shaded crevices under the cement path leading to her front steps. At the turn of spring, they would send out fresh green, heart-shaped leaves through which the dainty heads of the sweet-smelling violets would eventually peep. She would pick a posy each year at first flowering and put them into a cut crystal vase which she kept especially for this annual ceremony. It was only after she had harvested the first-fruits that I was also allowed to pick some.

Other favourites of Auntie Grace's from her homeland were mayflower, whose name always intrigued me, blooming as it did, draped like a bride in creamy-white petals, in August, and winter jasmine, which, also curiously, bloomed all year round. Unrestrained, the winter jasmine's branches radiated out from its roots in every direction, forming a circular fountain of yellow flower embellished arches, shooting up into the air, then arcing gently back down to the ground. Auntie Grace also grew blue hydrangeas, which were highly prized – blue being a colour not represented in the palette of native Australian bush flowers.

Our front fence was constructed of a wooden frame over which diamond-shaped chain-link fencing wire was strung. I suspect that all the fences had been erected by the original property developers, as so many of the same style of fence still bordered

---

£10. The scheme was devised to help develop Australia and reduce the pressure of rebuilding Britain's infrastructure after the war. It ran from 1945 to 1972. My godmother was something of an enigma to me. She spoke a different 'lingo', calling trousers 'traws' and talked about there being 'narry a skerrick' of things.

most of the properties. Where they had not rotted, fallen down, and been removed completely, or replaced with the more fashionable wide, white timbers of the 'ranch-style' fence, or the butterfly magnet that was a lantana hedge, most houses along our street were still fronted by a fence like ours. The side and back fences, although a different construction (being made of wooden palings), were also common to all our neighbours' boundaries. The only variation seemed to be the addition of side or back gates: some neighbours sharing them, and others not.

When town water was connected, Auntie Grace and Uncle Arthur took the necessary disruption of fitting an inside toilet as an opportunity to remodel and extend their modest, two-bedroomed house. Because their side water tank obstructed access for the builders, the fence between our properties was taken down and the builders brought their equipment and materials through our back yard. As a result, sadly, we lost the funny little wooden gate half way down the yard by which we would go to visit Auntie Grace and she would come to visit us.

Before the remodelling was done, Auntie Grace had a bathroom with a deep, enamel tub which I used to help her clean with abrasive cleaning powder called 'Vim'. The tub was so deep, I could not reach the bottom, so I used to climb inside, scrubbing around and around in circles, trying to erase my own footprints. Eventually, Auntie Grace would take pity and lift me out of the bath and rinse off both my feet and her bath with water from the tap. I expect I was more of a hindrance than a help.

Unusually, Auntie Grace also had a shower underneath her house, in a small boarded room with concrete for its floor, next to the tank and the washing machine with its customary cement rinsing trough. When her extension was done, this was all removed along with the rainwater tank.

The removal of the side fence would eventually allow a gang of us to use both back yards as a softball pitch. The ball was often belted from our yard, over Auntie Grace's, and landed in the long grass at the back of the shop, two doors up, also unfenced. Between all the neighbours, poor Auntie Grace and Uncle Arthur ended up with only their front fence and half a side fence, but no others! The fence between ours and Auntie Grace and Uncle Arthur was not replaced until after their passing, many years after I had left home for good.

We had another neighbour, who lived on our downhill side: an elderly lady called Mrs V. She shared my lichen fence. Her house was considerably older than ours, but had been maintained to a high standard over the years, so although it was a small cottage, new owners extended it as needed into the home it is today. Originally, it had only a front room and one bedroom which opened out onto a long side verandah looking downhill towards the creek and the ridge beyond, as well as a small kitchen and bathroom at the back of the house.

By the time we children next door came on the scene, the side verandah had rotted and was dangerous. We were not allowed to go out on it. I did, however, sneak out through the double doors in Mrs V.'s bedroom onto the springy boards one day and bounced them up and down, but the thought of falling straight through and onto the ground far below sent me scarpering pretty quickly back inside.

There were three verandahs on Mrs V.'s house – one at the front which had been enclosed and was used by the next occupants as a bedroom; one at the side which was condemned to be removed; and one at the back, from which the stairs descended to the back yard. Mrs. V. had a huge clump of bananas growing down the back by the sump (see page 54) and a chook pen (chicken coop) with bantam hens that supplied her with eggs.

Under the back and side verandahs she grew delicate ferns and hanging plants in baskets. In these baskets, scattered about randomly, I would find small, green glass leaves with holes in the top. They absolutely mystified me and searching for them amongst the many baskets occupied a lot of the hours of my long days. I realise now they may have been jade leaves from a twisted wire tree, like the real jade trees growing under the verandah where they were hidden. I wish I had kept them.

Under Mrs V.'s hanging baskets were a variety of succulents and cacti which bloomed with the most vibrant orange and cerise pink flowers imaginable. One of them – a moon flower – put forth flowers which opened and faded the same night. Its precious blooms were ghostly white and when I was older, I grew one of these cacti in a pot on my back steps and sat and watched it all night as its single bloom opened. Its wan petals peeled back one by one until they were all fully opened and then, without a moment's hesitation, began to turn back onto themselves and fade away. I was mesmerised by its beauty and vulnerability, and the nature of its opening – alone in the steely moonlight – was quite poignant.

Where the bottom of the wooden frame of our front fence had rotted, the wire, no longer being restrained by the 'u' shaped nails that had held it in place, curled upwards and left long, gaping holes where cats or dogs (or any other creature that was so minded) could squeeze through. Not that a cat or dog would have to go to such trouble, as all three of the old rusted metal gates on our wire front fence were left permanently wedged open as far as they would go.

There were double gates at the lower end of the front fence where our car would enter the property and drive down the side of the house. Although there was room to park it under the house, my father would park the car horizontally across the back yard so as to be able to get enough traction on the dewy grass slope to depart the next morning. 'Under the house' was always full of things other than our car. Usually it was home to the most part of some other car which was waiting to be repaired or broken up for scrap.

Although there was grass growing on our footpath, it could not survive the punishment meted out by car tyres crossing it twice a day, and the ground there was packed hard and gravelly.

Many happy hours were spent, sitting cross-legged and bare-footed in the dirt on our driveway, sifting through the gravel in hope of finding a diamond or a sapphire, an emerald or a ruby. Apart from sparkling chips of quartz crystal, my most prized finds were interestingly shaped pieces of shatterproof windscreen glass. I studied their clean geometric lines, turning them around and around to induce a lovely aqua colour to appear in the concave curve of the broken edge. These were my precious gems for which I designed, in my imagination, spectacular pieces of jewellery into which they would be set to glorious effect.

There were no proper cement car tracks on our drive, and since our house was built on a very steep hill, there were many times all of us would be called upon to help push the car (one of a series of three (iconic) grey[11] FJ Holdens my dad owned) back up the side of the house and onto the street after the summer rains had turned the ground into a slippery quagmire. In the years to come, tired of the seasonal car-rescuing drama, Dad would sink a series of breeze-blocks into the ruts the car tyres had made so that it was no longer necessary to park cars out on the footpath or in the street when it rained.

One of a series of three (iconic) grey FJ Holdens my dad owned.

Parking a car outside our house was particularly perilous. The hill was so steep there was serious danger of handbrake failure, and cars had been known to career down our street, shoot over the main road at the bottom, and a dirt service road below that, then on into the virgin bushland that lined the creek on the other side (after which the road, 'Creek Road' had been imaginatively named).

[11] Everything from the fifties – cars, furnishings, linoleum, or 'lino' on the floors, internal house paint – seemed to be grey.

Once this happened to a young mother who had parked her car outside the shop and popped inside for something or other, leaving her toddler son inside the car. Slowly, the car began to inch forward, gaining speed as the downhill slope of the street began to increase. By the time the car had reached our house, all that I saw was a flash of glass and metal as it shot past like an express train, down towards the main road. The poor mother, Mrs. M., was running along behind, utterly hysterical, screaming, "My baby! My baby!" The shopkeeper was running along behind her, and all the shouting and screaming brought the neighbouring housewives out to their front fences to see what was going on.

"My baby! My baby!"

Fortunately, the car shot across Creek Road just at a point in time when none of the usual cattle trucks, or other cars, were passing, and eventually nosed-dived into the long grass on the other side. The unkempt grass was so long and thick, it acted as a safety net and brought the car to a relatively soft halt.

The shopkeeper, Mr M., having outrun the lady, wrenched open the car door and grabbed the screaming toddler from the back seat, handing him straight to his sobbing mum. "He's ok, he's ok," we could hear Mr M. say, as a little head with a mop of curly ginger hair appeared over his mum's shoulder. All the other mothers, who, by now, had rushed out to help, were left standing by, crying tears of relief.

For this reason, when having to pull up on the hill outside our house, a large chunk of timber was left in the gutter, or on the footpath, with which to 'chock' one wheel of the car. If the chock wasn't there, the front tyre would have to be turned hard in towards the gutter, but this may have damaged the tyres, so was not ideal.

The gates to our driveway were never closed (except on one occasion when, being a conscientious child and suddenly realising that gates were fixed into fences for a reason, I duly pulled shut and latched all three of the gates on the front fence. Upon my father's return that evening, expecting the gates to be in their customary position, he drove straight into them in the dark. Suddenly, the reason there was a large dent in the wrought iron of one of the double gates became clear to me. It was impressed upon me that I was never to close the gates on the driveway again).

Neither was the wrought iron gate to the pedestrian entrance to the house ever shut. Like its counterpart, it too was rusted, with little scraps of peeling paint, various colours, representing a few attempts to tidy it up. I remember it being very plain – disappointingly functional – with straight metal rungs and no fancy scrolls, such as were sported by other gates in the street. The fact that it couldn't fulfil the only function for which it had been created seemed to make its predicament even more pitiful than its appearance. It hung permanently open, except for the times we children took it into our minds to stand on it and swing it back and forth, relishing its rusty squeals of complaint.

Next to the gate was a battered old metal box hanging limply from the fence. This was the letterbox. It was made from galvanised metal and had a slit opening at the front, facing the street, and a lid which could be raised from the back to retrieve the contents the postman would push inside. I believe it may also have had a coat of paint at one time. Nobody must have sent parcels in those days, as the letterbox could only take letters. The postman would come each day, riding on his bicycle, and blow his whistle if a delivery was made to the box. I expect if there was ever a parcel to deliver, a note would be left inside the letterbox and the parcel could be collected from the actual post-office down at Mt Gravatt Central.

When the old fence was eventually replaced by a new wall, which I will speak of shortly, the letterbox was accommodated within the blocks of the wall. A metal plate with a slot for letters marked the front and an opening flap which could take a padlock (but didn't) was positioned on the back. It looked much smarter than our previous letterbox on the outside, but the reality was that the workmen who fixed it into the wall left large, rough lumps of mortar inside which scratched the skin off any knuckles that came into contact with them in the course of retrieving the post. The new letterbox was also lower in the wall and dark inside – a perfect home for the venomous spiders for which Australia is well-famed, hidden from the sight of the owners of probing fingers.

The postman, or 'Postie', never came to the door. Posties were a brave breed of man – always men – who delivered the post faithfully in every weather, and did not quake at even the most potentially injurious attacks to their persons. Alongside them in the line-up of suburban super-heroes stood the paper-man and the milkman.

While the paper-man infuriated the neighbourhood dogs by cycling into their territories, slinging a rolled-up newspaper over the fence and then scarpering as quickly as he had come, the milkman was exposed to even more danger by having to come to the front steps of the house before depositing daily milk orders and removing empty milk bottles. Milk money would be left out weekly next to the empty bottles, to pay for the delivery, and such was the nature of the community, that it was never interfered with, at least not in 1960s. Fortunately for them, the deliverymen who serviced our house in those days had to do battle with neither a dog nor a squeaky, rusty front gate!

On the street side of our front fence with its obsolete gates was a sloping footpath which had been tamed by a previous householder, grassed over, with most of the stones removed, and having two trees planted on it which provided the neighbourhood children with a great opportunity for imaginary play. The tree on the higher side of the footpath was a rather sad and straggly poinciana, and the one next to it, downhill, was an equally scruffy-looking jacaranda.

Each year, when the jacaranda flowered, we children would gather up the fallen blossom, poking our fingers deep into the mauve trumpets and making 'witches' fingers'. This game was played enthusiastically by our neighbourhood friends and we would squeal with excitement as we chased each other all over the footpath, up and down the hill and across the street, taking turns to be the 'witch'.

Our footpath sloped in two directions, both down the street, and also down towards our house. It had been planted with fine, low-growing couch grass – very slippery when wet – and we spent many happy hours sliding down it on sheets of thick cardboard from packing boxes we pilfered from behind the shop. To get the best slide, the flattened box would be positioned at the top of the slope, as close to the dirt street as possible, and each child would take a run-up and throw themselves onto it, grabbing hold of the edges as it took off down the slope.

It seemed so fast and furious when we were young, but looking back at the slope of the ground as an adult, I wonder that we thought it was so thrilling. The greater thrill was to build a go-cart and shoot down the hill at breakneck speed. We would have to go over to the next street along for that, as our hill was too steep even for the most fool-hardy of us to go-cart down it more than once!

Making go-carts out of wood, rope and whatever wheels could be found, then racing them against other go-carts, was a very serious business in the neighbourhood. It required some considered scavenging for parts and the forbidden use of Dad's tools. Although I was rarely allowed to participate in the design or building of a go-cart (being a 'girl') I would be allowed to drive it once it had been made. They were not the most robust of contraptions and the wheels were always falling off at speed, sending the central plank of wood nosediving into the ground and the driver shooting headfirst over the front of it into the dirt and gravel road.

My most abiding memory of go-carting was the day we stole the big wheels off our baby brother's pram and went go-carting down our hill. I don't know how we survived the activity in one piece, but when Mum came out and saw what we were doing, we got her angriest 'Wait 'til your father gets home!' – assumed to be an empty threat, as he rarely came home when we were still awake. However, as luck would have it, this time he did come home and for the only time in my memory, we three were lined up as he sat on a kitchen chair, put us over his knee, and ceremoniously spanked our bottoms, one by one.

We were 'dealt with' in order from oldest to youngest. Dianne took her punishment first, then ran crying down the hallway to our bedroom. Greg was next, and he slunk off to his room without a word. I was last, and, never having been smacked in such a fashion as this, I was full of trepidation at how painful it was going to be. Surprisingly, not very. Perhaps my father took pity, as I was the youngest. I rewarded him by running down the hallway to my bedroom shouting, "Nah, nah, didn't hurt!" He made no attempt to chase me to smack me again, as I feared he might. I think he may have been too busy trying not to laugh out loud.

I remember with sadness the day the council came and cut down the trees on our footpath. One day they were there, and the next they were gone. Only the roots were left to rot in the ground. I remember asking Mum why, but I don't remember her answer, if there was one. However, it became self-evident quite soon after, as I was afforded the daily diversion of standing on the front fence, or swinging on our squeaky, rusty gate, watching council workmen firstly grading our street, and then sealing it by laying down smelly black tar and rolling gravel into it with an almighty, thundering steam roller. To my child's mind, the sights and smells were almost apocalyptic, and prophetic of many such changes to which I would bear witness in the coming years.

Up to that point, the street outside our house had been quite inadequate in bad weather, with a lot of bare earth and loose stones. The ground on which the estate was built was largely clay and shale. When it rained, the steeply inclining streets and lanes became so slippery with muddy water that they became impassable, and cars could not be driven uphill. My dad would tell stories about how he would turn into the street at the bottom of the hill and manage a few yards, then unceremoniously slide, tyres caked in sticky mud, back to the main road where he had started.

The residents of the lower end of our street would have to approach their homes from the top of the street where the incline to the top of the hill was more gradual. Cresting the highest point, they could then drive (or roll) downhill, taking great care not to slide into trees or telephone posts, or overshoot their driveways and continue to slide on down to the main road. Although Creek Road was a major route, it was sealed only with a narrow lane of bitumen, with wide dirt shoulders on each side. If motorists did not get their manoeuvres quite right, it would mean a round trip, back through Mt Gravatt Central, to the top end of the street again – a distance of a few miles.

In years to come, when it came our turns to learn to drive, the challenge was not so much the driving test, as learning to negotiate our own driveway from either direction. Coming at it uphill, the car could either stall or undershoot the driveway. Approaching from the top of the hill, the car would have to be held back in a low gear while braking hard, or there was a risk of overshooting the driveway and then having to drive around the block again.

It was thought to be a great leap forward to have the surfaces of the local streets properly sealed with new bitumen. Not only was the street made safer, proper curbs now marked the edge of the footpath, which channelled the flow of rainwater into the echoing chambers of underground storm-drains. Up to that point, torrential summer downpours would send water gushing down the slope of the front yard and under our house, spewing over the concrete retaining walls like a mini Niagara Falls. From there, it would continue down our back yard and into the neighbours', where it would squelch up between bare toes from under the grass in a slippery, muddy ooze.

In addition to this significant improvement to our daily lives was the laying of concrete footpaths along Creek Road: the main road leading down to the shopping area at Mt Gravatt Central. This parade of shops, banks and offices was known to the locals as 'the terminus', or 'the termo', because it was the last stop, or terminus, of the tram service into Brisbane City Centre.

This meant crossing the main thoroughfare through Mt Gravatt Central

The tram line had been extended to Mt Gravatt in 1951 and the service was discontinued in 1969, in favour of a better developed, city-wide bus service. Up until then, a family called 'Howatson' had run a local bus service which picked us up for school on the side of Creek Road. Some of Howatson's buses were housed in an ancient corrugated iron shed on Creek Road, between Raffles and Grenfell Streets (the same place as we collected Bauple nuts, page 117).

The shed was no more than corrugated iron nailed to a wooden frame which was open at the ends, and even then, the iron sheets were rusted and falling off. It was flanked on both sides by two grand old Queenslander houses. One house sat between it and a small chapel on the corner of Raffles Street and Creek Road, and on the other side, another old house was positioned on the corner of Grenfell Street and Creek Road. The latter was a particularly elegant, sprawling house with steps leading up to its wide, covered and ornately decorated verandah that were so intimidating, they seemed to challenge passers-by with, "Come on in and climb me if you dare!"

Getting to school on Howatson's bus in the morning was a risky business. Passengers would squeeze precariously into a straggly line on the dirt shoulder of the main road at the bottom of our street and hope the bus came before a smelly truck full of cattle going to the abattoir down at Bulimba went by.

As well as school children, there would be older girls and ladies heading into the city to work in typing pools or accountant's offices. The bus only went as far as Mt Gravatt Central, where passengers would alight on the footpath outside Barry and Robert's grocers, then cross the main thoroughfare to the centre of the road to board the tram. This meant crossing Logan Road, which was comparatively busy, to take the tram the final two stops to school.

It did not take us long to figure out that if you got on the tram at the rear, you could alight at the school before the conductor had time to get to the end of the tram to collect your fare. If timed successfully, it would deliver a bonus of three-pennies-worth of lollies after school. Furthermore, if you walked all the way to school instead, you could spend both fares, bus and tram, on such delights as eucalyptus drops or cobbers[12].

It was very sad to see the trams go, but the increase in car traffic had made alighting from them into the centre of the highway far too dangerous. The faster we go, the less patient we get, and where people had been cautious and willing to stop for tram passengers before cars ruled the roads, sadly, that courtesy and sense of communal responsibility seemed to be eroding as the pace of life sped up.

Prior to the upgrade of the roadways, the footpath along Creek Road had been no more than a well-worn dirt path, trodden back and forth by shopping mums and school children carrying oversized brown pressed cardboard boxes called 'ports'. With adjustable leather straps and a flip-top lid secured by a metal clasp, these cavernous boxes were carried on schoolchildren's backs to distribute weight evenly and promote good posture. However, they were very cumbersome when it came to playing on the way home. Besides which, they never seemed to transport anything much more to school than a lettuce and vegemite sandwich, wrapped in greaseproof paper, in a brown paper bag with twisted corners.

---

[12] Eucalyptus drops were square, opaque white, hard-boiled sweets, which tasted more like medicine than sweets, but we liked them anyway. Cobbers were cubes of hard toffee dipped in milk chocolate.

They never seemed to transport anything much more to school than a lettuce and vegemite sandwich.

Chapter 3

Traffic

Fences are erected to establish boundaries. They mark the extent of the territory to which we lay claim, to which we belong, and in which we feel safe. They keep those who don't belong to our group out, except with our permission, and keep our youngsters and our animals in.

That's the theory, anyway. In reality, every man and his dog were free to cross our fences unchallenged, and they (both) regularly did. The reason? The shop two doors up from ours was the only local grocery supplier for a very long way around. It was known by the name of the proprietor: 'Thursby's' or 'Mulligan's'. When a proprietor bought it who didn't really fit comfortably with the local clientele, it reverted to just 'the shop', almost as a statement of non-recognition of its owner.

All the world was free to use our property as a shortcut to the shop. It was very convenient that our fence was broken down at the back corner (or maybe that was why?) and our front gates permanently open. Distances in Australia are quite vast, (I think they have longer miles!) and it could be a long walk wherever you need to go, especially if it required traversing hills. Neighbourhood stores were few and far between – possibly miles apart, even in built up areas – and residents accepted without question the need for foot travellers to go 'as the crow flies' as much as possible to reach their destinations.

It was not only our yard which was used as a cut-through for convenience. Having emerged from a gap in the fence and treading the diagonal line across our back yard, the locals, mothers and children alike, would then cut across Auntie

Grace's front yard to make their journey as short as possible. When Auntie Grace's fence was in a state of disrepair, we would also cut across her front yard, ducking under her graciously bowing poinciana, and saving ourselves the five or six extra steps it would have taken to go out of the front gate, onto the public footpath and then back down to the shop door!

People came from far and wide through our yard to get to the shop. Often I didn't even know who they were, appearing from under the acacia bushes at the corner of our broken fence and making their way up our back yard in search of a packet of cigarettes and a cold bottle of Coke. It was as if they had some mysterious internal compass which they followed, like elephants to their graveyard: a sort of communal consciousness which permitted trespass on the understanding that nothing in the properties through which the traveller passed was interfered with. When new people moved into the neighbourhood, the short-cuts through their yards were generally respected.

When our lichen fence neighbours moved away, another elderly couple moved in and wanted to upgrade their fences. In order not to make themselves the pariahs of the neighbourhood by blocking the cut-through, they custom built a diagonal section across the corner especially to preserve it. However, since the supporting railings of the new fence all joined at the corner post as usual, we now had to jump the fence, or crawl under it to get through. That was fine for us as children, as we could fit underneath. It was not so good for the mums who had to be very athletic to jump uphill to get over the top. Puffed from the exertion, travellers would exchange their greetings on the way to the shop, offering them a moment to catch their breath, as they would be in a hurry on their way home, not wanting their cold drinks to get hot, or their chocolate bars to melt.

I wore mine to our aunt's wedding.

In the days before cars were common, and certainly before housewives and mothers had access to them, standing on the fence in the front garden, or hanging around while my mum poked at the ground between her rose bushes with a stick (an activity she referred to as 'doing outside') would afford many interesting social and commercial encounters. There were ladies coming up the hill heading to and from the shop who would stop and natter for a time and girls running errands for their mums, but, more intriguingly, there were commercial traders who would drive down the hill selling goods from the backs of their vans. They were called 'tinkers' and sold everything from saucepans to children's clothing. Whether they had any true association with a real gypsy community, I have no idea.

Once my mother purchased two little tunics from a passing tinker – one for my sister, Dianne, and one for myself – which consisted of a pleated skirt sewn onto a calico (unbleached cotton) bodice which, collarless and sleeveless, would be topped by a blouse or jumper. Mum (who was a very skilled needle worker) knitted matching pastel jumpers in a twisted cable pattern for us to wear over the top of our pleated skirts. My jumper was an apricot colour; Dianne's was green. I wore mine to our aunt's wedding. Dianne and I both had white raffia handbags which had spiralling mother-of-pearl periwinkle shells sewn on the front, especially for such a special occasion.

One particular day on which the tinker came with his van was most memorable because, as Mum was in the process of making her purchases, the wind whipped up a 'willy-willy' on the dusty footpath where we were standing.

A willy-willy (also called a 'dust devil') is a spiralling funnel of dust and debris which touches the ground like a mini-tornado, picking up gravel and leaves and hurling them high in the air. The footpath outside the shop, where this willy-willy formed, was so well trodden, it was never anything but dust and stones – not a blade of grass could survive the customers' footfall. As a result, this particular willy-willy had plenty of ammunition to toss into the air, including discarded lolly-pop wrappers and smelly, dead cigarette butts!

Another mobile trader, whose display shelves perched on the back of a flat tray truck, was the fruit and veg man. He sold eggs, seasonal fruit and local vegetables from the back of his truck, all displayed neatly as if they were in a market stall on the High Street. He did not come down our street out of courtesy to the owners of the shop: there was an unspoken agreement not to compete with the shop for trade, but he did drive up and down the neighbouring streets and our friends' mothers would often take advantage of the opportunity to stock up on these perishable items. We also used to have an occasional visit from rough, overall-wearing men who collected scrap metal in a truck with a big, open, flat tray at the back, and of course, the tune of the ice cream van could be heard coming from streets away, giving us plenty of time to pester Mum for some money.

For those mothers who trod the path down to the big shops at the terminus, for a small fee, brown paper bags filled with their purchases could be delivered by van to their front doors, often arriving before the lady of the house could walk back home. For this reason, the front door of our house was left not only unlocked, but actually open, to allow the bags of groceries to be put inside, out of the burning sun. If a bar of ice cream[13] was in the delivery, the driver could actually be asked to put it in the freezer compartment of the fridge!

Before Coles New World opened up on Creek Road, Mum and I would go shopping at the terminus on most days for groceries. The place I loved to go best was the large Barry and Roberts grocery store, where the tram line began. There was a slightly more modern grocer over the road called 'the BCC' (Brisbane Cash and Carry) which co-joined with a sort of department store called 'Walton's'. The BCC had an internal stairwell at the back which went straight into a carpark and delivery area behind, then down further to the field through which the creek ran from behind the back yards of houses on Bothwell Street. The slippery clay drop in the grassy bank that marked the back of their carpark was replaced the concrete

---

[13] In those days, ice cream was sold either in blocks wrapped up in silver-foil lined cardboard wrappers, or metal tins which, when the ice cream was finished, lived out their remaining years under the house, stuffed full of rusty nails or nuts and bolts.

steps which are there now, in a small retaining wall going down into Bothwell Street.

A footpath ran along the side of Walton's which went from Logan Road all the way up the hill to Grenfell Street, near Orb Lane, and it was a real challenge to run up its steep slope into Raffles Street, the first street it crossed, without stopping. This was our least preferred route home from school, as climbing the hill along this footpath left even the fittest of us gasping for breath.

I was always pleased when Mum chose to shop at Barry and Roberts because they had their vegetables lined up in open wooden crates with sets of scales hanging above them, all shiny silver. They would swing back and forth under the weight of the produce being plonked into their removable scoops to be weighed. This grocer was more old-fashioned than the newer BCC across the road, and that made it somehow more appealing to me.

I remember choosing potatoes for Mum out of a huge crate covered with the dust and dirt that had fallen from the round, brown vegetables. Hunting for the biggest one in the box, I chose a huge knobbly potato that looked like several joined together. I struggled to get it out, finally holding up my mud-caked prize with both hands, and was most put out when Mum rejected it and refused to put it in her brown paper bag with the others. A lady who worked at the shop graciously intervened and, producing a knife from her deep overall pocket, split my giant prize open straight down the middle to expose a big hollow space inside.

She leant down and whispered to me, "It's what's inside that counts." That was a lesson learned!

Mum and I would trudge up our hill to get home, Mum with her string bag in hand. She would have dispatched the groceries to be delivered before buying meat at the butcher's on the way home so she could she could carry it back herself. Her string bag, which, when empty, hung limply from the doorknob on the back of the side door, could expand to hold an enormous amount of goods. Sometimes we would see the delivery van coming back down the hill, the driver having deposited our purchases safely in the side porch before closing the back door behind him. It was always rewarding, having expended the last ounce of energy and willpower dragging tired feet up the hill to our home, to find a bag with iced buns, juicy oranges or fruit cordial inside the front porch, waiting to be unpacked.

Two more frequent visitors to our street were not so exciting to encounter. In fact, if I should be caught out in the yard when they arrived, clattering and shouting down the hill, I would hurry inside to be out of their way. They were 'the garbos' (the garbage collectors, who emptied our household bin) and the 'dunny men' (who removed and replaced the toilet pans from the outhouse in the back yard). Even thinking about them now has me feeling slightly panicked. I can almost hear the banging of metal on metal and their shouts to move on. More of them later...

Our poor, dilapidated front fence was not to last many years beyond these days. With the proceeds of a small inheritance, the rotten timber, rusted wire and gates were swept away and a chunky, grey breeze-block wall put up in its place.

My mother was most concerned that the workmen did not disturb her roses in the process, but in the days immediately prior to the work commencing, during one of my ambivalent inspections of Mum's flowerbeds, I noticed something new growing beneath

a rose bush which made my eyes pop open in surprise and wonder.

There, nestled in a small hollow in the lumpy clay soil, was the sweetest and most vibrantly coloured flower I thought I would ever see. Its leaves were dark green and shiny, serrated at the edge and lobe-shaped, and its single flower had petals of the most vivid purple and yellow, like tiny cups of gold on royal velvet, and a striking black centre. I don't know where the seed had come from, but I now know that I had found a single heartsease which had randomly taken root in Mum's flowerbed.

Not knowing that it was possible to lift the tiny plant and pot it, I prayed that it would somehow survive the digging of the foundations of the wall, but sadly, it disappeared beneath the turned earth and I never saw another one again until I immigrated to England as an adult and identified it from memory.

It was a delight to find my little childhood friend had a name (several, actually) and I still make a point of scattering heartsease seeds around the flower beds and plant pots of my home in homage to that brave, solitary flower which had been sacrificed to the march of modernity in the form of home improvement.

Although the crooks to support new metal gates had been fitted into the finished wall, no new gates were ever hung.

My mother had several flower beds in the front garden which she tended as best she could, always having to rely on natural rainfall, as our water supply was limited to the amount of rainwater which could be captured in the water tank at the back of the house. Prior to our neighbourhood being connected to the municipal water and sanitation system in 1967, water was an especially precious commodity and could not be spared to water flowers, grass or trees. If there was a drought, the tank which collected and stored our water would empty and no one had any water to spare. There was no back-up source except prayer.

For this reason, the fruit trees which were routinely planted in the back yard (flowers in the front, fruit at the back) were planted close to something called 'the sump'. The sump was an area of stinking, boggy ground, halfway down the yard, where the pipes that took waste water away from the house finally ended and the dirty water, and its contents, would rise to the surface like a gloopy geyser of vegetable peelings, animal fat, and grey soap scum. Next to the sump were planted banana trees, a lemon tree and a large weeping willow, all making the most of the abundant supply of water and nutrients the sump provided.

Every local child had enjoyed that old weeping willow.

When town water was laid on, the willow tree was cut down to prevent the roots breaking into the new pipes in search of water. I remember coming home from a day out with the family who had moved in on the other side of my lichen fence after Mrs V. passed away, to find vegetative carnage down that side of our house. Huge tree branches lay across the grass – fresh yellow wounds weeping and sawdust and leaves scattered far and wide. I remember that I actually cried with shock, horror, and then anger. I experienced a wave of emotions, from a terrible sense of betrayal and loss, to helplessness that my old and loved friend had been brutalised in my absence and would soon be removed forever from my world. In some real way, I could sense the willow's distress. All this in the name of progress. My parents could not understand my bizarre and extreme reaction, and neither could I explain it to them.

I imagine just about every local child had enjoyed that big-hearted weeping willow. Rough, springy, branches diverged from the trunk fairly close to the ground, making it strong and good to climb. Clambering as high as we dared and grabbing fistfuls of its long, leafy boughs, we would launch ourselves out into the yard and swing as far as we could, leaping off at the farthest point and flying through the air until gravity inevitably yanked us back to solid, unyielding earth. It was a great accolade to be acknowledged as the person who flew the farthest.

We all shouted, "Tarzan!" as we swung out into the air, and we *were* Tarzan for a moment in time. Despite the pain of our inglorious landings, we would be scrambling back up for another go, faster than the next child could launch.

Further casualties of the coming of town water were the fruit trees. They stopped producing edible fruit. The pith of the citrus fruit became thick and the segments dry and tasteless from lack of moisture. Every so often, in an attempt to address the problem during drought conditions, Mum would lay a hosepipe uphill of the trees and allow the water to trickle slowly onto their root systems overnight. Instead of drought being my mother's problem, she now made it the problem of the entire city of Brisbane!

The tank in which our water was collected and stored sat at the rear of the house, against the back wall. It was a huge storage tank made from galvanised corrugated iron, the same as the roof, but concrete-lined and enclosed at the top, except for a small hole into which the downpipe from the roof guttering was fed. Near the base of the tank was a single bronze tap, not too close to the bottom, to allow space for sediment to build up without contaminating the clear, sweet water that would be drained off for drinking.

Pipes were connected from the tank which fed directly into the kitchen and bathroom, so all our drinking and bathing water was soft, untreated rainwater. To heat the water, further pipes were diverted from the tank into a hot water storage cylinder under the house, which then fed heated water to the hot taps in the bathroom and the kitchen. We had no shower in our bathroom, so water was conserved by sharing bath water between four children. Whoever had to go last into the bath probably came out dirtier than they went in.

The tap on the water tank was the most precious piece of metal a child could ever lay their chubby hands on. If the tap was left open by a negligent child, the whole tank's life-sustaining contents would drain out upon the ground and be lost. Tanks that had taps which dripped could easily be identified by the lush native ferns and moss which would spring up around the stumps supporting their stands.

It was not only careless children who could commit this most heinous crime of wasting the tank water – wild parrots such as cockatoos and galahs would often learn how to turn on the tap in a bid to find water to drink, but never quite got the hang of how to turn it off it again.

The only way for our water tank to fill was to catch the rain that fell on the corrugated iron roof of the house. It would drain down the corrugations and into the gutters, working its way around to the downpipe that finally directed it through an opening on the top of the tank which was covered by a fine mesh screen (to keep out small dead animals). Into the cool, dark, echoing interior it would trickle – or gush, as the case may be during cyclone season. The tank itself rested upon a large, wooden-slatted platform, raised up on wooden stumps to a comfortable height to provide access to the tap.

When the city council finally connected our street to the town water supply (and after the wailing lament from every housewife about the hardness of the 'town' water died down) these tanks were rendered obsolete, served notice, drained and removed. They were deemed to be a health hazard, being a perfect breeding ground for mosquitoes which could host tropical diseases like malaria and dengue fever.

I cannot remember how our tank was actually removed from its stand, but taking down the stand and knocking down the old dry toilet in the back yard was a project that demanded the joint effort of several of the men of the neighbourhood, since indoor, flush toilets had now been accommodated in every home. The neighbourhood dads would go to each other's back yards to help with their dismantling and removal, unless only the wooden toilet box was removed and the outhouse turned into a shed for garden tools. The lady over the street from us, Mrs L., had her tank drained and dismounted, but then rolled to the rear of the yard, where it sat for some time: a useful covered storage area, and a great place for the local kids to play!

Galahs would often learn how to turn on the tap on the tank.

Chapter 4

Fruits and Flowers

My mother was an avid gardener and her fingers were certainly 'green'. She grew a wonderful array of flowers in our front yard, against all the odds, and took particular pleasure in collecting as many varieties of rose as she could.

Mum loved long-stemmed tea roses, especially the ones that produced enormous, blood red, velvety blooms. Each rose would be planted a regimented space apart along the inside of the wire front fence. No two roses of the same colour would be planted next to each other. She had yellow roses and vibrant orange roses, as well as white and various shades of pink. Her greatest prize, however, was a rose called 'Blue Moon' which was actually a grey/mauve colour and smelt like Fry's Turkish Delight. This seemed to me to be a thing of wonder – a flower that smelt like a chocolate bar!

Alongside her prized roses, Mum planted many other interesting flowers in the raised concrete beds that ran along the front wall of the house. I whiled away many hours studying the forms and colours of her flowers, imbibing their various scents as they bloomed and faded in their due seasons. I also used to nibble on their astringent, fleshy leaves and petals, and, before he was whisked off to school, my brother and I would gather up their dead, hollow stalks and light them with forbidden matches and pretend to smoke them, like cigarettes.

Being a very literal child, I tended to take everything I was told to be gospel truth, and reasoned out some questionable conclusions of my own based on the few facts I had been given. Mum warned me of every flower, bush or tree in the garden that was toxic to eat, and so, I figured in my childish mind, all the others must be edible. Consequently, I went about testing this theory, sampling each one, to see which did or did not make for an appetising snack.

Flowers or shrubs that exuded milky sap, according to Mum, were poisonous, and although I could pick the flowers, I was to be careful not to ingest any of the sticky, white sap that may cover my hands. This blanket warning covered a huge number of the exotic plants that were to be found growing in our yard.

Along the side fence, in both our yard and Auntie Grace's, grew many varieties of the beautiful, but very poisonous, Mediterranean oleander. The scruffy, blade-leaved shrubs sent out clusters of flowers with either single or double petals, in colours ranging from white and pastel pinks, to deep, burgundy reds. Each little lipstick-shaped bud was twirled up in its sepals and as the flower opened, it would untwist, like a boiled lolly being pulled out of its wrapper. They had fascinating seedpods, long and thin, like the ancient sharpening steel Mum used to sharpen her carving knife. When the seed pods had dried out, turning from green to brown, they would split open down a side seam and fluffy seeds would burst out, to be whisked away on the breeze.

Although they were pretty to look at and played host to stripy caterpillars and their magical silver pupae, the oleander bushes were to be avoided at all costs. Even the dead branches, having been broken off or pruned, were not to be put into the 44 gallon metal drum that served as our incinerator. The smoke, apparently, would also contain particles of its deadly neurotoxic sap (although I am sure I have a vague memory of trying to whittle these soft branches into whistles, as they can be hollowed out and cut easily when completely dried out).

The same warning was given about the glorious allamanda vine which, at one time, had draped its sunshine-yellow, bell-shaped cups across the roof of the outhouse. Various shrubs Mum grew which originated in South America and the islands of the Pacific Ocean fell into this 'toxic' category and some, although not so dangerous, could cause some skin irritation if the flowers were handled or picked. Such was the pretty, pale blue plumbago, which also spent some time adorning the side of the outhouse. Some of the vines, also having hairy leaves and stems – protection against insect attack – could cause an irritating rash on the exposed skin on arms and legs. This was the case with the choko vines that also grew at one point on the side of the outhouse. On reflection, a lot of plants seemed to take turns growing on the sides of our outhouse.

Chokos are a type of edible gourd from South-east Asia which grow fruit in abundance, providing free vegetables for households where money was never in such abundance. The fruit, which was used as a vegetable, was similar to button squash, shaped like a large pear, and pale green in colour. It was covered with thin, shiny, bumpy skin. The fruit would split sideways into two halves to reveal a large, rubbery seed, or 'stone'.

Preparing chokos for the pot was a tricky business, as the sap, like that of gourds in general, is alkaline and will strip the skin from the cook's hands. Having sacrificed a few good layers of epidermis, the dinner-maker would slice the choko into segments and boil it until soft, which took only seconds, then drain it and mash it with a fork. The pale green flesh would instantly disintegrate into a watery, tasteless slush, to which copious amounts of butter, salt and pepper would be added. It came as no surprise to see the choko vines on our outhouse being replaced by the equally robust and prolific (but much more flavoursome) passionfruit.

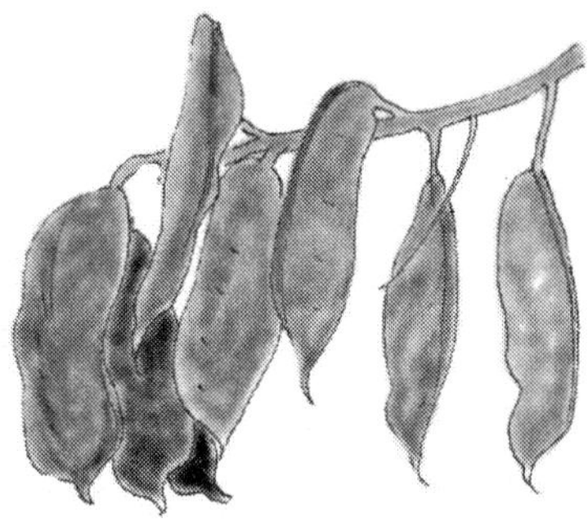

Brilliant yellow acacia shrubs grew down at the back fence, where the long grass had been cleared. They produced thin, bean-like seed pods that I was warned never to touch. In fact, many of the trees produced poisonous seeds in pods, such as the (Kentucky) coffee tree with its wisteria-like clusters of yellow flowers, which produced large, pendulous, flat seedpods. When fully dried, they would become woody and their seeds inside would rattle, making excellent maracas. Wily schoolteachers would collect them for their music lessons, as the whole class (yes, almost 50 of us) could join in with free musical instruments! The hard little black bullets that were the seeds of the scruffy canna lily were also to be avoided, as well as all berries and all mushrooms, toadstools and fungi.

With my infantile powers of deduction, I reasoned that any flowers, leaves or fruit of the trees that were not on the poison list, must be safe to eat, so I experimented on them all. A good selection of 'safe' flowers remained to sample, which included hibiscus (too slimy), begonia (too sour), nasturtiums (too peppery) and rose petals (too boring!). Fresh peppermint was good and I ate a lot of that (on one occasion, including half a green caterpillar).

As well as the aforementioned citrus fruits, passionfruit and bananas, there were a lot of fruit and vegetables that would grow by accident, included papaya (paw-paw to us) which could spring up at an astounding rate and fruit prolifically, watermelon, and anything else that poked its head out of the compost heap and presented us with fruit. Whatever seeds went in, so the fruit came back out. The compost heap produced such delights[14] as giant Queensland Blue pumpkins (squash) with their thick greyish green skin and vibrant gold flesh, and a selection of tomatoes, capsicum (peppers) and cape gooseberries (physalis).

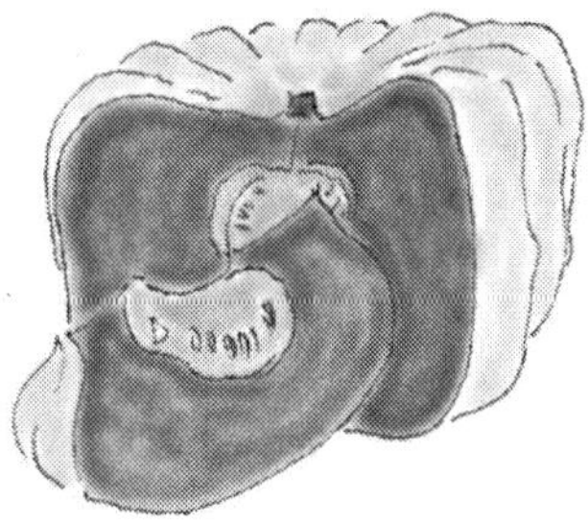

We did have a mango tree down near the back fence, but getting a ripe mango off a mango tree is an art nobody in our house seemed to acquire – not even my green-fingered mother. She used to wait until the mango was almost full sized, but still unripe, then tie a brown paper bag over it to keep out the fruit flies which would lay their eggs in it at the first opportunity. This course of action was tantamount to doing a rain dance. Within days, the paper bag would be sodden and torn and fall off the fruit. Nobody cared after that, as if you really needed a mango, someone else would have hundreds of them lying on the ground, free to anyone with a bucket.

[14] I say 'delights'. It was every child's duty to refuse to eat pumpkin except, possibly, if it was roasted until it was black and sweet and served with a leg of lamb. Either that, or disguised in scones.

Another common fruiting tree in our yard, which was to be found in most yards back then, was the banana tree – although it isn't really correct to call it a tree. It is actually a type of grass, although some people even take exception to that classification and insist it is just a herb – albeit a very big herb. Bananas don't grow from seed. They send up new plants around the base of a mature one, which are called 'suckers'. They do not have woody stems, but their 'trunks' are made up of concentric layers of their own leaves.

In Queensland, the state where we lived, we were called 'banana benders', because of the numbers of bananas which grew there, and the fact that somebody had to put the bend into the ripening fruit! In fact (some knowledgeable adult informed me) the banana gets its bend because, when it is forming at the base of the flower, it bends as the flower bends towards the strongest light. So bananas growing on the side of a hill are all supposed to bend to face the same way. I don't know how this can be true, because they all bend in towards the branch on which they are growing.

Bananas are interesting fruit to grow, as they all grow together on a long hanging branch, and ripen from the top down. The fruit are called 'fingers' and a bunch of them joined together at the back is called a 'hand'. A branch holds several layers of hands surrounding it. When the bananas are still green, the whole branch is cut off and hung somewhere cool and safe, like underneath the house, so the fruit can be picked as it ripens piece by piece from the top to the bottom.

I remember long branches of bananas hanging under our house and eagerly awaiting the fruit becoming ripe enough to eat. We and our mother were at odds about exactly when was the right time to eat a banana. She seemed to think bananas shouldn't be eaten until they were yellow and began to develop black spots on their skins – then they were truly ripe. We thought any time we felt like it was the right time to eat the bananas – even when they were green, floury, rock-hard and sank to the bottom of our stomachs like lead.

I don't remember the fate of the banana trees. Perhaps they were part of the clearance of 'down the back'!

Our back corner neighbour, Mrs M., had a very unusual type of fruit growing in her yard which would also ripen bit by bit, but from the bottom up. Its proper name is monstera deliciosa, known more commonly as the 'Swiss cheese' houseplant. We used to call it 'monsterio'. The fruit started out inside a huge, elegant, creamy-white cowl, which withered away to leave a thick green fruit shaped like a large cucumber, with hexagonal shaped armour plating. When the segments of the fruit ripened, the green outer skin fell away with the slightest touch and creamy flesh surrounding sharp little black seeds were exposed. If you didn't mind the spiky little seeds, the white flesh tasted like a tropical fruit salad.

Mrs M. also had a lovely mulberry tree which was covered in fruit in its season, when it would have a gang of purple-mouthed (and purple-footed) children gathered around underneath it, feasting on the juicy, sweet, black berries. Mulberry pie after tea when there was a glut of fruit was a great treat.

A particular tree which overhung my lichen fence produced fruit which was very similar in appearance and habit to ordinary cherries. My mother said it was a Brazilian cherry tree, so I figured, if it was a 'cherry', it couldn't be placed on the 'don't eat' list with a great deal of conviction. It was worth the risk of sampling its luscious looking orangey-red, cherry-sized fruits. The somewhat oval-shaped fruit, with a scalloped outer skin, had stalks like cherries, skin like cherries, flesh like cherries, pips like cherries, but certainly didn't taste like cherries! It was both sharp and bitter, and eating too many of them gave me stomach ache, but eat them I did.

Most flowers and shrubs in our yard were there, however, simply to be enjoyed. No month of the year went by without there being something special and intriguing poking its head out of the soil or casting off its protective sepals and bursting out into the sunshine. One such exotic beauty which grew in the front yard was a tiny-budded deep-pink and purple fuchsia. No other front yard I had ever peered into sported a fuchsia bush. It reminded me of so many tiny ballerinas in gaudy tutus, or ballroom dancers wearing gowns of multiple layered pink and purple tulle.

Another annual floral treat came in the form of a clump of giant, pale pink, autumn-flowering croci called 'colchicum' which sprouted from somewhere deep underground in the scrappy grass next to a telephone pole on the footpath. Where they came from, nobody seemed to know. They were certainly not native.

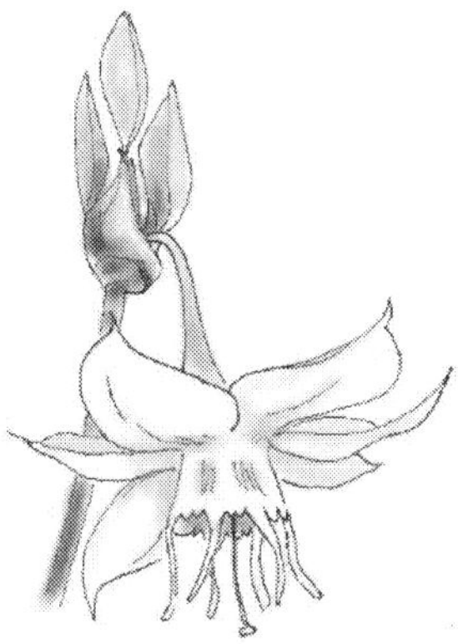

Delicate beauties whose origins I did know was a clump of highly prized, exquisitely formed, translucent white Eucharis lilies that had been transplanted from beneath the front steps of my grandmother's (my mother's mother) big old Queenslander house. They were almost like white daffodils in that their appearance each year heralded Easter, and it was eagerly anticipated. As much care as possible was afforded them, to encourage them to flower, to establish and to reproduce. Eventually, sadly, whether through adverse weather or soil conditions, or attack by pests, they seemed to disappear from their corner of the front garden bed and were relegated to memory.

I have a curious memory of one plant Mum took exception to and tried to remove from her flowerbeds. It was the pretty, but persistent, caladium, or 'elephant's ears', which had spread into every nook and cranny around the concrete borders at the front of the house. A variegated variety, with pink, white and green stripes, I never understood why it caused my mum such annoyance, until one day, as she was digging up another patch of it, she muttered something about them 'being here when we got the house'. Aaaah!

Of all the flowers that bloomed in our yard, my favourite by far was the stephanotis, or Madagascan jasmine. All varieties of jasmine have an exotic, heady perfume by which they can be identified. Its cousin, the delicate, creamy gardenia, also had a place in Mum's front yard.

The creamy-white clusters of tubular, star-faced flowers which the stephanotis produces makes it popular with brides. Appearing each year from amongst their waxy, crisp, oval-shaped leaves, ours would put on a grand starry burst on the palings at the side of the house. I would stand and breathe in its intoxicating perfume until it seemed my whole body was filled up with its comforting warmth. But this dark-leaved vine, which entwined itself torturously around the palings on the underside of the house, did not just produce flowers of outstanding fragrance and beauty. An equally significant contribution it made to my home world was that it fed the larvae of the black and white 'common crow' butterfly.

The common crow butterfly would also lay eggs on the oleander, but more of the larvae could be found on the stephanotis vine, so I assume it preferred the taste of those leaves. The funniest thing about the stripy caterpillars of this black and white butterfly is that, instead of also being just black and white, they are black, white and orange. I used to wonder if it was not a mistake that they did not hatch out of their chyrsalises as orange and black monarch butterflies instead.

When butterfly season was about, I would watch the stripy 'convict' caterpillars munching away furiously along the edges of their host leaves until they were ready to pupate. They would then attach themselves to the centre of the underside of a large, oval stephanotis leaf, hanging upside down, and slough off their striped skin, exposing a layer that would soon harden into the shiny silver armour of their chrysalis. At this point, I would gently pick the leaf from the vine and suspend the hardened chrysalis over the mouth of a suitably sized jam jar, the two ends of the leaf resting on either side of the rim.

There it would sit, being monitored daily, until black lines began to scribe their patterns across the silver plating. The emergence of the adult was imminent, and, if I was really lucky, I would catch the process in time to watch the chrysalis slowly splitting down its back and the crumpled black and white wings of the adult butterfly begin to emerge.

Slowly, silently, the delicate wings would unfurl and the insect would gently waft them to and fro, as if to dry them, or find the feel of them. At this point, I could cautiously place a finger in front of the creature's delicate legs and it would trustingly oblige by stepping onto my hand. When my curiosity was satisfied, the butterfly would be ceremoniously returned to the outside world: to the stephanotis vine, to continue the natural cycle of its life.

Slowly, silently, the delicate wings would unfurl.

Chapter 5

Bugs

It is hardly surprising that, seeing as the land on which the new housing estates were being built had not that long ago been either virgin bush or farmland, the new 'people houses' became the adopted homes of much of the area's wildlife.

Our place was only two houses and a road away from a strip of undisturbed bushland through which the creek ran, from the foot of Mt Gravatt and out towards the bay, following the line of a valley between two rising ridges. Although only seven miles[15] from the centre of the city, we teetered on the edge of the bush and the occasional farm paddock waiting to be engulfed by the mass of house-building spreading like syrup on a hot pikelet.[16] Like it or not, the native inhabitants of the bush still visited us. Our yard was always teeming with life – gastropods, insects, arachnids, reptiles, amphibians, birds and mammals – some welcome, some definitely not.

Firstly, let's get the nasty ones out of the way.

Taking their place at the top of the list: flies. Flies came in lots of sizes and colours, but they were always present and always a nuisance. They were always somewhere near, buzzing about, looking for things to crawl all over and contaminate. They would crawl on faces, up noses and into open mouths, if given the chance. They laid their eggs everywhere they could and

---

[15] Seven miles is about 11 kilometres.

[16] Pikelets have lots of different names, depending on where they are being made. To us, they were round, spongy circles of batter made from eggs, flour and milk, about five inches (12 centimetres) across and tossed on mum's ancient cast-iron frying pan until golden brown.

our house offered near constant opportunity for maggot infestation. Maggots in the garbage bin, maggots in the outside toilet, maggots in the drains, fruit fly maggots in the mangoes on the mango tree. It didn't matter how often I encountered maggots, they never ceased to revolt me.

There were a few defences against flies – some more successful than others. Many of the householders at that time were discovering fine mesh screens that could be put up against the windows so they could be kept open to the fresh air, but most of the flying invaders kept outside. Since our windows opened outwards, they did not easily take screens. Mum had to deal with the worst of the flies by hanging a coil of sticky fly paper from the kitchen ceiling which caught them when they alighted upon it. By the end of the day, it would be covered in half-dead, still buzzing, black blobs.

If fly paper was not agreeable, there was always fly spray. Before fly spray began to be sold commercially in aerosol cans, it was sold in tins which had to be screwed onto a spray pump. These pumps were made of brass, or tin, barrel shaped, with a long tube attached which housed a plunger. Some gardeners still use this type of spray pump to control pests.

Fly spray was noxious and the droplets fell quickly onto all the surfaces in the house, so it wasn't ideal to use around food, children or babies. Neither was it a long-term solution. It would kill the flies that were present when it was sprayed, but as soon as it dropped from the air, the next hoard of flies were free to invade.

The last resort, and most ineffective weapon against flies, was the fly swatter. Purpose-made fly swatters could be bought (a sort of mesh square on a stick), but many a persistent, irritating little fly would meet its maker on the end of a rolled up newspaper!

It must be said, though, that even flies are not all bad. Most were nasty little black annoying pests, but it could be quite exciting to find a large bluebottle, with its peacock-coloured abdomen – especially after it had died on the windowsill and could be studied at leisure.

Joint first on the nasty list with flies was mosquitoes. Although flies were disease spreading (contaminating surfaces and food and laying eggs that soon turned into white, wriggling, revolting maggots), mosquitoes could also spread disease, like malaria and dengue fever. Most often, however, where we lived, they just injected people with an anticoagulant so they could suck out their blood, leaving a nasty, raised and painfully itchy lump the next day.

With the amount of standing water around in which their larvae grew (because of rainwater tanks) there was always an army of mozzies waiting for lights out to set out on their nocturnal blood harvesting campaigns. The best defence available came in the form of the mosquito net. Mosquito nets were made from a fine cotton mesh, woven into little hexagonal cells, which were draped from wooden frames like rectangular halos fitted to the headboards of the beds. By day, the net was gathered up and fed behind the headboard, but at bedtime, it was pulled out and draped all the way down to the bottom of the bed, and hung all down the length of the side.

Mozzie nets were very effective at keeping mosquitoes away at night. They would buzz away on the outside of the net, doggedly bombarding the hexagonal holes of the mesh to gain access to their potential victim inside. I would frequently slap them between the flat palms of my hands from the inside of the net, using only their incessant buzzing as a guide to their exact location. In the morning, I would find brown blobs on the net where, should I have been successful and they had been squashed, some other unfortunate person's blood had created a stain on the white gauze.

There were some disadvantages to having mosquito nets as well. Once in bed, the net had to be pulled down from outside or the sleeper would spend the night waking up with the mosquito net tickling their nose. It was also difficult to get out of bed from under a mosquito net in the dark. They tended to get tangled up in sheets and pyjama bottoms.

If mosquitoes were bad before bedtime, Mum would resort to breaking out a 'mozzie coil' which was a coil of fibrous matter which, when lit, would smoulder away slowly, filling the air with smoke which kept them at bay. Someone once told me they were made from pressed horse manure, but I don't believe that at all. Our Uncle S. once gave us some new-fangled citronella-infused wax candles with wind resistant rope wicks for outdoor use, which smelt lovely – and worked a treat!

Number three on the disgusting insect invaders list must be cockroaches, or 'cockies'. Now, there are two types of cockies – the nice ones that are large, white native parrots which behave like clowns, and love to say 'hello' and have the back of their necks scratched, called 'cockatoos'. They are lovely. The other sort, is the malevolent, armoured-plated, flying muck and disease spreader, the maker of nightmares, which is the cockroach.

Cockroaches, like flies, also come in all shapes and sizes. Some are tiny and flightless, infesting the dark corners and cracks of a house, such as under the sink, hidden and unsuspected, until the homeowner turns on the light in the middle of the night and sets hordes of the secretive scavengers scuttling back to their netherworld.

The malevolent, armoured-plated, flying muck and disease spreader, the maker of nightmares, which is the cockroach.

On the other end of the spectrum is the giant flying cockie which, erratic and belligerent, flies in through an open window in the dark and dive-bombs anything and anybody in its way. Should it startle an unsuspecting homeowner, causing him or her to fling their arms about to chase it away, these giant cockroaches take umbrage and set about harassing their victim by flying repeatedly at their head and chasing them in terror from the room.

There were a collection of other very nasty bugs which would make their way into the house at times, according to the weather, or the season of the year. For example: there were tiny, black ground fleas which would come up into the house when seasonal rain flushed them out of the ground. There were also bird lice which would come down the internal walls of the house in search of blood when their hosts – sparrows nesting under the eaves in the roof – had raised their brood and abandoned their nests. Dad had a novel way of warding off bird lice infestations – he would put our old ginger tom cat 'Big Red' up into the loft space to get rid of the nesting birds!

Ants were generally benign, but would infest the house if any foodstuff was left on the work surfaces – especially anything sticky, like jam or honey. There would be a single, black line of these busy little creatures snaking all along the work surface, out of the window, down the outside of the house and then disappearing into a crack in the cement path outside.

Although our little brown town ants were harmless, in country areas further afield, there were mounds of huge, angry, reddish brown ants called 'meat ants' which would swarm out onto anything that came near to the nest and start biting it viciously. An assortment of other types of ants could also be found in the grass which would sting if disturbed and, of course, there was the scourge of every wooden dwelling: white ants, or termites.

Termite infestation is a very serious risk to wooden houses. Termites, or white ants, will work away, eating the timber from the inside out, leaving a shell of layers of exterior house paint as the only thing taking the weight of the rest of the building. In order to minimize the risk of termite attack, the thick wooden stumps which were used to raise the building up from the ground would be topped with galvanised metal caps which looked like upturned plates. The termites could not go past them and into the main body of the building. Over the years, these thick wooden stumps would rot in the ground to be replaced by concrete or metal posts, or the house would be shored up on bricks.

There would sometimes be swarms of midges, or sand flies in the yard, with their nasty little bites, and of course, no house (or outhouse) would be a home without daddy-long-leg spiders in every corner and behind every door. Although having an extremely toxic venom, the daddy-long-leg's mandible is so small, it cannot puncture human skin, so, unwittingly, we were kept safe from these potentially lethal arachnids that shared our home.

There was one danger we fortunately did not face.

There was one danger we fortunately did not face in the area in which we lived, and that was the bite of the notorious red-back spider. We had a huge variety of spiders which spun their webs from plant to plant and post to post around the yard, but the extremely venomous red-back was not amongst the crowd when I was small, although it has now re-established itself in the area.[17] Neither did we fear the deadly funnel-web, living too far north for its habitat.

We did, however, have trapdoor spiders which would make their little cave-like tunnels in the mossy banks of retaining walls, sitting at the mouth and waiting for unsuspecting night insects to fly within reach. Their eyes would shine in the beam of a torch like pinpricks of light, and as they were approached, all their traps would slam shut and the little lights that were their eyes would disappear.

---

[17] Not that red-backs spin webs from post to post – they make a messy sort of nest in the corners of fences, underneath flowerpots and in guttering.

Another variety of spider, which was very common in our yard, particularly as the days grew cooler and autumn approached, was the St Andrew's cross spider, with its legs paired up and resting in the shape of a cross and bright yellow and white stripes across its abdomen. It had a very clever way of weaving a white zig-zag cross into its web and it would sit in the middle of it, its paired legs following the lines of the cross as they radiated outwards.

The most vivid memory I have of an encounter with a spider happened when I was down at the creek after a particularly long rainy spell. The grass had grown long over the path and then been flattened down by the rain. It was still knotted up in itself and dripping wet. All my efforts to make progress were directed at the path in front of me, until I felt a strong, sticky string attach itself across my face. Looking up, I found myself nose-to-nose with the biggest spider I had ever seen in my life (a golden orb-weaver – as big as my outstretched hand). It was sitting in the centre of its web, surrounded by the black blobs of its prey, all wrapped up in silken thread, and about hand's width in front of my eyes!

It lurched towards me, the disruptor of its web, and, heart thumping madly, I quickly back-tracked, well out of its way. I had to go back the way I had come and find another way around so I could continue my journey home, but I paid a lot more attention to what was in front of my face instead of what was in front of my feet.

I stayed away from the creek for some time after that.

I found myself nose-to-nose with the biggest spider I had ever seen in my life.

But enough of the nasties!

There were also many beautiful and harmless insects (beetles in particular being a favourite of mine) which either lived with us permanently, or visited our home seasonally. If they lived with us all the time, they were left undisturbed. If they visited us seasonally, they were welcomed with great delight.

The first of these seasonal visitors which comes to mind is the beautifully adorned Christmas beetle. It is so called because it usually arrived just before Christmas. At that time of year – summer – the temperature and humidity was very high and the windows of our house would be left wide open in the hope of catching the merest stirring of the moisture-laden air. By night they would come, swarms of them, attracted by the light in the kitchen, left on after our bedtime. While frantically bombarding the single, incandescent bulb, the beetles' silvery wing-cases would click rhythmically against the light's shallow metal shade. We could hear the 'tap, tap' from our beds.

In the morning, the kitchen table would be covered with the corpses of so many of these shimmering armoured warriors, we would have to clear them away before we could have our breakfast. The hard shell casing that protected their delicate tissue-paper wings was silvery-white with a rainbow effect on it, like petrol on water. Any beetles that were still alive would be on their backs, waving their brown legs in the air and trying to catch hold of something to help them turn themselves back upright. We'd reach out a finger and let them take hold with their sharp little hook-like claws and then pick them up and take them outdoors.

There were very many varieties of beetles around our yard and another particular favourite of mine was known as the 'stink bug'. Flamboyantly coloured in metallic blues, oranges and greens, they would congregate together in large numbers and any significant disturbance could induce them to release a foul smelling odour. Once one had let off its stink, they would all join in, and stink they truly did! I learned to handle them very gently and would allow them freedom to roam all over my hands and arms as I studied their intricate patterns and variety of stunning colours. No two were ever the same.

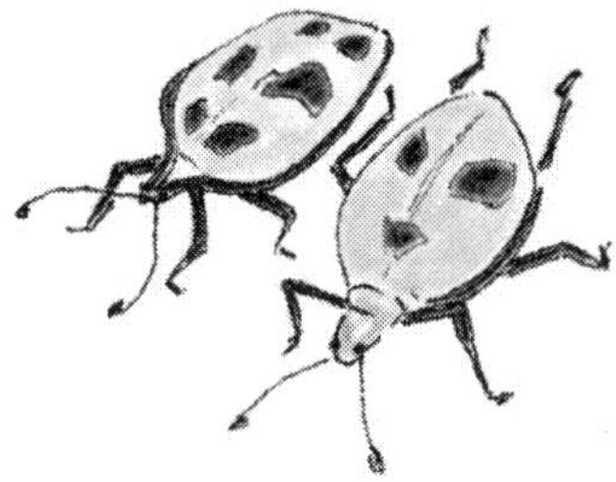

From small bugs, to big bugs, the variety was endless. Delicate little green praying mantis would occasionally alight on fences and window sills, and sometimes even on our clothes. They would sway from side to side and hold two legs together in front of their faces, as if in prayer.

Their larger cousin, the stick insect, was not so delicate. Growing up to a whole foot in length,[18] knobbly, spiky and brown, they would hang from the branches of our grapefruit tree, absolutely still, and when I went rummaging about in the bitter-smelling leaves to see how big the grapefruit were growing, they would suddenly move and frighten me half to death, so well camouflaged would they be. They could actually fly, and the wings that folded up and lay along their long backs were incredibly fine, like the sheerest of tissue paper, with a delicate lace pattern of spots and stripes.

Other insects abounded in our yard, both by day and by night. The clover in the grass was host to a thousand happy, busy, buzzing bees, going about the business of collecting sweet

[18] One foot is about 30 centimetres.

nectar to take back to their hives for their young. I never saw a hive anywhere, so I have no idea how far they had come.

I was taught to respect bees – they had a job to do, and if I didn't disturb them, they would not sting me – so I was told. This Mexican standoff generally went quite well, until, being a child that chafed at the restrictions of wearing shoes and always preferred to be barefoot, I accidentally stood on one in the clover half way down the back yard. The burning sting I received, despite my toughened heels, taught me to be a lot more careful about where I put my bare feet.

Grasshoppers and crickets were permanent residents in our yard, more often heard than seen, as well as cicadas that sang out their grating zithers all day and night in the sweltering summer heat. Moths came by night – mostly small and dowdy, grey and dusty. However, some were magnificent, white, and large, with fanned antennae and various spots and stripes. They were velvety and comforting – plush – like a gentlemen's smoking jacket, or had incredibly intricate lace patterns, like a flamenco dancer's fan. The larvae of the moths were often as stunning as the moths themselves, like the caterpillars of various hawk moths, which were big and juicy, with textured patterning and shockingly huge, fake eyes, or even delicately green with fine white diagonal stripes.

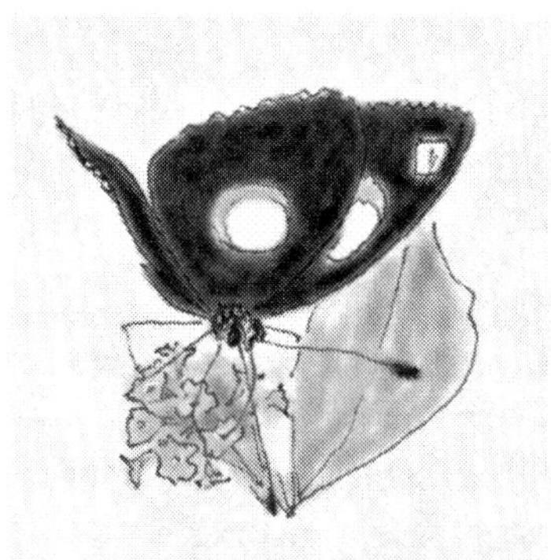

Perhaps the queen of all the insects in the yard would have to be the butterfly. So many varieties, so many shapes and colours, they brought pleasure every time they were seen fluttering around their favourite shrubs that lined our back fences. I would watch them extend their long, fine proboscises into the very centres of the flowers from which they fed, and wait for the thrill of spotting the vibrant patterns and colours of their wings as they casually opened and closed them as they rested. Some butterflies had more colour on the backs of their wings than the front, which was an interesting sort of reverse.

Butterfly eggs could be found on the underside of the leaves and their larvae would be given away by the appearance of scallops around the edges of the leaves which hosted them. Perhaps the most striking butterfly in terms of coloration was the peacock, with its distinctly sinister double pair of eyes designed to scare off predators by looking like something absolutely huge and best avoided, which were painted on all four of its velvety wings.

Some black beauties in the butterfly world were the eggfly butterfly, with its giant white and fluorescent purple eyes on its wings, and several types of swallowtail. Some butterflies had delicate colouring which looked like lace on their wings and there was one butterfly whose wings were completely transparent, as if made of cellophane. If I had to choose a favourite, it would be the 'Art Deco' blue triangle butterfly with its black wings and gorgeous, vibrant aqua-blue triangles on its wings.

The house in Bothwell Street at the end of the footpath next to Walton's offered the most wonderful place to find every different variety of butterfly in the area. Its side boundary, which ran along the lane, was made of a high lantana hedge. Butterflies and bugs swarmed all over it and it hummed constantly with the sound of diligent bees going about their nectar gathering duties. Children and adults alike would stop to inspect and admire its insect population.

Not all butterflies paraded around like carnival divas. Some were quite plain, and moths, which were usually plainer, could be quite vibrantly adorned. The way to tell the difference between a butterfly and a moth is that butterfly wings are closed and raised upright when the animal is at rest, while moth wings are open and lay flat in line with their abdomen and thorax.

Having looked at a few of the insects that I used to enjoy finding in the yard, we must move on and look at some of the other animals that called my home their home.

If I had to choose a favourite, it would be the 'Art Deco' blue triangle butterfly.

Chapter 6

Reptiles, Birds and Furry Things

Now spiders and insects can be all very fascinating, and some of them even beautiful, but they don't make very good pets. Once a butterfly has hatched, it is quite determined to escape to the great outdoors as soon as a window is opened. Sporadic attempts to catch and tame crickets, or grasshoppers, seemed always to end in failure, so my attention turned to some of the inhabitants of our yard that were more suited to domestication (apart from our cats and the dog from next door who thought he lived in our house anyway).

The most successful of my endeavours at taming the native wildlife involved lizards. The rising sunlight from the east fell full on the back half of my lichen fence. On cold winter mornings, a cross section of the resident lizard population would often be found bathing themselves warm in the early morning rays on the railings of the fence, camouflaged against the weathered grey palings. Taking great care to creep quietly up on them, with a quick hand and the expertise that comes only with a lot of practice, I would often bag myself a baby bearded dragon.

Bearded dragons are wonderful – they make lovely pets. All covered with tiny spines, they would blend perfectly into the rough, bleached wood of the old fence until disturbed, then they would take off at lightning speed, disappearing into the rustling grass. A lizard hunter had to be quick to catch them under their hand – and I was. When they realised they couldn't escape, they would flatten themselves against the fence railing, making their bodies as big and as round as possible.

Once caught, these fierce looking, but quizzical little lizards would be easily persuaded to sit on my shoulder and accompany me to school, where they would be the centre of attention at 'little lunch'.[19] They may even make it to the end of the day, but having no way to properly care for them, and knowing in my heart of hearts they belonged outside, they would be released in the evening into the back yard in a vague but sincere hope that they would have enjoyed making my acquaintance so much, they would be there the next morning to do the same again. Sadly, I was doomed to perpetual disappointment on that score.

One boy who lived down on Creek Road actually did manage to tame a bearded dragon and saw it grow from babyhood to full adulthood – nearly three feet,[20] including its tail! The fearsome-looking beast was enormous, but the boy would walk it along the road with a string tied around its spiny neck and it never seemed to object. When he pulled the string, along it would come, keeping pace with him as he went. He would hold it up to show us and if it did get annoyed by the unwanted attention, it would open its huge jaws to reveal an almost fluorescent yellow mouth and tongue, with a row of little, needle-sharp teeth. How I envied that boy his amazing pet!

---

[19] At primary school, we started school at 9 am. There were two breaks – 'little lunch' in the mid-morning and 'big lunch' at midday. We finished at 3 pm.

[20] Three feet equals one yard, just shorter than one metre.

How I envied that boy his amazing pet!

I once witnessed a baby bearded dragon perform a feat which defied the laws of gravity. Down at the creek at the bottom of our street one day, I disturbed a small bearded dragon as I made my way along a path in the long grass. Startled, and seeing no way of escape other than straight across the water, that is exactly what this little lizard did. It took off across a wide, slow flowing lagoon-shaped stretch of creek, up on its two back legs, racing along on tippy-toes and whipping its long tail back and forward behind it. I was startled at first, then amazed as I realised what I had just witnessed – a lizard, walking on water!

There were lots of other types of lizards that would take up residence in our yard. Another dearly loved occasional squatter was a huge, lumbering blue-tongue, so called because of its thick, bright-blue coloured tongue, which it would poke out slowly from between its scaly, prehistoric jaws. Blue-tongues are a type of skink – a very big one.

Blue-tongued lizards do everything slowly. With short legs, and covered in shiny, smooth scales, they lumber about, their bodies oddly truncated with a short, thick tail. They live in cracks underneath houses – cracks underneath concrete, cracks underneath downpipes – and it is a privilege to have one take up residence in your yard.

Ours would live under the cement front steps and come out on occasion, trundling about in a leisurely fashion, looking for insects and grubs to eat. We usually knew when it was out and about, because the cat would be seen in the yard going a bit mad, jumping around in a slightly demented fashion with its back fully arched and its fur standing up on end.

Old Big Red never quite knew what to make of the blue-tongue. He would pounce at it, but when it just ignored him, Big Red would rapidly retreat and rethink his attack strategy. The lizard just lumbered along, back to his home under the front porch steps, completely unfazed, and never seemed any worse for its encounters with Big Red.

Blue-tongues are really well loved as pets because they are so mild mannered; they can be tamed straight from the wild. They can be caught (even by a granny with a zimmer frame) and picked up without any fuss or aggression. Or they can be enjoyed from afar, just left alone to go lumbering about their business.

From the giants of the skink world to the midgets – the dearly beloved little skinks that lived on the fences and under the house were ever-present and always brought a smile to my face. They were sleek, and they were fast, dark grey, with two lovely long silver streaks down their backs, a metallic blue tinge to their tails, and busy little eyes, watching every movement from every direction. They were hard to catch, especially while trying not to cause them any damage in the process – but I did manage to catch them on occasion.

When one of these slippery little skinks got worried enough, it would shed the end of its tail in the hope of distracting whatever enemy was harrying it long enough for the rest of the lizard to escape. The end of the tail would lie wriggling on the concrete like a worm – an equally appetising prey. Then the skink would run off and simply grow a new tail. These harmless skinks would sometimes come to live inside the house, particularly in the kitchen, where they could set up residence safely under the fridge, or under the cupboards, and come out to feast on toast crumbs and fruit flies.

As well as reptiles, our yard was home to a few amphibians – frogs and toads. Frogs seemed quite rare, but on occasion, after a lot of rain, we were treated to the company of the tiny green tree frog, which was considered a real privilege. Hidden under large leaves and brilliant green in colour, they were white underneath with vibrant yellow toe pads, and, with very little persuasion, they would sit quite calmly on the end of your finger. Larger green frogs with white underbellies would occasionally make an appearance out of the downpipes, which directed rainwater down to the ground, once they were no longer needed to send the flow into the water tank.

Wriggling black tadpoles were always plentiful down in the creek. We would often catch them and bring them back to put into an old fish tank we had lying about under the house, or a giant pickling jar. Safely secured in their new home and elevated to eye level on a tall, three-legged stool that lived in the side porch, we would watch them with great interest as their tails disappeared and the little stumps erupting from their sides began to grow into legs as they developed into adults. Goodness knows what happened to them after that. I don't remember there being any plague of frogs in our yard.

The amphibians' visits we could well have done without were the nocturnal ones made by cane toads. Cane toads were introduced into northern Queensland from South America in the 1930's by cane farmers in an attempt to deal with the grubs of the sugarcane beetle that were ruining sugarcane crops. Unfortunately, the cane toads did not provide a successful solution to that problem. They were not able to reach the grubs in the cane from the ground, and not able to climb up to get the grubs either. Having no natural predators, they went about, happily overrunning every watercourse they encountered with their oversized spawn. They spread very rapidly down from the cane fields and all over South-East Queensland. Any attempts at predation by higher species was killed off (literally) with their poisonous neck glands. They remain invincible, but apart from that, they are just unbelievably ugly!

My first up-front and personal encounter with a cane toad came about as a result of our toilet being in the back yard. Before we children were dispatched off to bed each night, we were all sent to the toilet, as we could not go after dark, which, even in summer, was no later than about 6.30 pm. However, the back door would always have its oversized black metal key left in the oversized black metal lock and a rather feeble old torch was usually (but not always) left to hand.

I shudder still, remembering the night I met the cane toad, in the back yard, in the dark. I had needed to go to the toilet when everybody else was asleep in bed, so, being quite brave (so I thought) and independent, I made my way down the dark hallway from our bedroom to the back door and, locating the torch, took myself down the back stairs and along the concrete path to the outhouse.

I shudder still, remembering the night I met the cane toad.

It was a chilly night and the grass was already wet with dew, but the concrete path was still warm under my feet. Chirp! Chirp! Bzzz-bzzz! I could hear the sound of the nightlife all around. Moths fluttering at the torchlight, mosquitoes buzzing, then … Plop! Plop! I froze. Only one thing could make that much noise as it moved across the yard in the dark. Suddenly, a huge cold blob landed on my foot. PLOP! I leapt out of my skin with fright! The biggest, ugliest, lumpiest cane toad I had ever seen had landed on my bare foot, its demonic eyes glinting red in the torchlight's impotent beam.

I turned tail and ran back to the back steps, leaping up three at a time, far out of reach of the evil, dinner-plate sized sentinel that was guarding the path to the outhouse. I'm sure, following this episode, I must have found more creative ways of answering nature's call during the night.

Visits to our yard by native birds were much more enjoyable events. Most of the resident birds were quite dull, colour-wise. We had a lot of brown and grey house sparrows, and plenty of pigeons – not the comical, fat, pink and grey wood pigeons that visit my garden in the UK and are always a pleasure to see, but the smaller, sleeker type of pigeon that is kept by enthusiasts because it will come home to its coop. Sometimes, we would hear the gentle cooing of doves, but they were not so common.

Imminent rain would be heralded by the robust laughter of the boisterous kookaburra.

The native birds tended to keep themselves to themselves, somewhere out in the bush. They could be heard on outings in the countryside, but rarely seen. Mum always enjoyed hearing the curlews, as it reminded her of her childhood home in Toogoolawah, a little country town up in the mountain ranges that form the Brisbane Valley. Whip birds were easy to identify, as they sounded just like whips being cracked. Another really delightful sound of the bush was the chime of the bellbirds – again, they chimed, just like the 'tink' of a glass bell. But none of these native birds visited my home.

We were lucky enough to have occasional visits from Australia's best known bird. Imminent rain would be heralded by the robust laughter of the boisterous kookaburra. One particular bird would come and sit, not in an old gum tree, as the song goes, but on the television aerial, and laugh away maniacally with the most raucous laughter.

"Rain on the way," Mum would say. My mother grew up in the bush and knew all the ways the farmers predicted the weather by watching the animals. If she saw a cow lying down, "Rain on the way." If she saw ants moving their eggs, "Rain on the way." If the glorious sunrise was touched with a rosy-pink hue – "Storms!"

Kookaburras, along with magpies and butcher birds, could be trained to come and take pieces of minced meat tossed to them in the air. Black and white magpies were another common sight, as were black crows with their petrol sheen. Well, crows were a common sound, anyway, with their long, lazy 'caw' that travelled for miles, inducing a sense of resignation and inevitable doom in the hearer.

The birds we really liked to see were the colourful ones. Each year, when particular trees were in bloom, flocks of gaudily coloured parrots, which both looked and acted like the worst behaved of clowns, would descend upon suburban yards, feasting on the nectar of the flowers on the umbrella trees, or bottle brush. We had a tree on the back fence which, for want of a proper name, we called the 'peacock' tree. It had springy boughs which were good to climb, with a cork-like texture in the wood. The flowers were red, a little bit like a giant pea flower, and looked like a peacock with its tail fully raised – hence our improvised name.

Flocks of rainbow lorikeets would fly in over the neighbours' roofs, descending in a swirling kaleidoscope of colour, and go mad over the nectar in these flowers. They would squabble and fight over the blooms, hanging upside down from the branches and screeching at each other, orange beaks clashing and wings madly flapping.

Flocks of gaudily coloured parrots ... would descend upon suburban yards.

Once, a young lorikeet fell prey to old Big Red, who, probably not being able to believe his luck, somehow managed to hold onto it long enough to get it back to the house, before dropping the poor, terrified bundle of feathers down a narrow crack between the cement path and the palings under the house. The bird screeched from its prison like it was being murdered, although I doubt Big Red could have managed to kill it, such was the fight it was putting up and the viciousness of its hooked orange beak.

I had been wandering about with a piece of toast, just about to leave for school, when I heard the almighty commotion. Racing down the steps from the kitchen, I found the bird, firmly wedged. I ran to get a towel to wrap it in, to protect my hands as I prised it out of its cement prison. I wasn't taking any chances with that beak! Big Red was very upset to have been robbed of his catch and darted back and forth, around and around my feet as I walked off with his prize.

Just a little diversion, since I am thinking about Big Red. He was born in our house, the biggest of a litter of three kittens, and grew to be an enormous ginger tom cat. He wasn't overly friendly, nor was he unfriendly.

He just turned up for food twice a day for a lot of years and hung about the place, sleeping here and there under bushes. One day, a concerned neighbour came to tell Mum that Big Red, who was well known in the neighbourhood, had been hit by a car down on Creek Road. He was dead and had been left lying in the gutter.

My mother, who professed to hate all animals, was saddened by the news, but went dutifully down to collect his lifeless body and bring it home to bury. She dug a suitably sized hole down the back near the incinerator, laid Big Red to rest, then went back upstairs and about her business.

A few hours later, there came a familiar yowl behind her as she stood working at the kitchen sink and, turning around, she found Big Red, presenting himself in the kitchen doorway, looking for his dinner. Mum almost fainted with shock, thinking she was seeing a ghost-cat, before realising she had just inadvertently buried a stranger's cat in our back yard!

Big Red had a history with birds. We once had a lovely yellow canary which sang its heart out with the sweetest tunes. One day, it somehow managed to escape from its cage and fly out into the yard, landing in a dishevelled heap in some bushes. I watched in horror as Big Red leapt out of nowhere and grabbed the poor bird in his mouth, taking off up the road with it as fast as he could. Assuming the worst, it seemed pointless to try to give chase, so I went back to whatever I was doing.

A few moments later, with a lot of shouting and hoo-haaing coming from up the road, Big Red leapt back over the fence, canary still hanging from both sides of his mouth, and dropped the lifeless bird at my feet. Quickly grabbing it from the lawn and shooing the cat away, I thought to myself sadly, "Well, at least you didn't get eaten."

To my astonishment, the little yellow bird fluffed up his feathers and started struggling to free his wings from between my fingers. I carefully secured him back into his cage, checked his seed and water, and kept an eye on him for a while. He was completely unharmed. That plucky little singing bird lived for many years after.

Another lovely pet bird which lived with us for a long time was a pretty pastel blue and green budgerigar which I caught in our back neighbour's yard. Hearing its call from our adjoining back yard, I tracked the lone bird into the branches of an enormous mango tree next door. Rushing to get a towel, I climbed the six foot[21] wire fence and then the tree, edging out as far as I dared along the branch on which the bird was sitting. I then threw the towel in the direction of the bird and to my utter surprise – caught it! I probably hadn't actually needed the towel. The little budgie was completely tame and came to me willingly, looking no more than bemused at the effort I had taken to capture him.

Even though budgerigars are native birds, when they have been bred in captivity and escape into the wild, other birds will often attack them. Wild budgies are normally protected by being in a flock. Solitary birds do not do so well, so it was a kindness to catch my little budgie and put him back into a cage to be looked after. He lived with us for many years afterwards.

Mum (who was known as 'Mrs Noah' by the neighbours as she was always being followed about by a train of animals) used to

---

[21] About two metres high.

say that it was not a good idea to have pets, as you get too attached to them and then it's upsetting when they eventually die. I think possibly she was right, but it didn't stop us from having a plethora of pets.

We searched and searched ... but no koala was to be found.

Although it may have been a common belief, many years ago, when I first arrived in England, that there were kangaroos hopping down Australian suburban streets, it wasn't actually the case. They lived way out in the bush. Neither did we have koalas living in our yard, as we didn't have the right type of gum tree for them to feed on. However, our friends from down the back came rushing up to our house one day to tell us there was a koala in the big gums that lined the fence between them and their side neighbours, the W.s.

We rushed, helter-skelter, down the yard and through the broken fence, past the wooden skeleton of a cabin cruiser their dad was building in their back yard (as you do), and down the side of their house to see the koala. We searched and searched the canopy of each enormous gum, but no koala was to be found. To this day, I am not sure whether they were just tricking us.

Possums were far more likely to set up home under the roof of a house or garage and if they did, it was almost impossible to get rid of them. They looked so cute – sort of like fat, fuzzy pussy-cats, but smelt terrible and were not at all friendly. Any attempt to catch one was like trying to get hold of a biting, scratching, fur-covered demon. They were certainly not as cute as their great big round eyes made them look!

In the 1970s, my friend W. (page 165) had a whole family of possums living in the gum trees alongside her house. Her mother used to feed them bread from the lounge room window, where they would come down the branches and wait for this daily treat. I think W.'s mum had a change of heart when the acrid smell of possums began to overwhelm the house and the yard!

They looked so cute, sort of like fat, fuzzy pussy-cats.

Chapter 7

Our House

Various aspects of our house and yard have already been mentioned, but I thought I would spend some time describing our home and its contents in more detail. There is a sketched plan of the house near the end of the book, on page 155.

Our house was built in 1948, three years after the end of the Second World War, during a building boom that was seeing much of the open farmland that was Mt Gravatt being subdivided and turned into residential streets. A Mr George Chester was responsible for much of the building, but I am not convinced that he was responsible for building our house. The style and building materials used were much more like the houses being built by the government Housing Commission, a few streets further down Creek Road from us, although our street was not on the Housing Commission estate.

Our house was built in the middle of two narrow plots of land, and therefore had two street numbers – 11 and 13. We used number 11 as our address. Our mother, who was very superstitious, would probably have refused to live at a number 13 anywhere, even if it had been 13 Buckingham Palace! The house was made of rough weatherboard, rather than the more stylish and smoothly finished chamferboard, and had been painted a most unusual turquoise colour, which had faded down to a powdery mid-blue by the time we lived there. Instead of concrete tiles on the roof, it had corrugated iron, painted silver, and the layout inside was very basic. It had not been designed with the comfort or convenience of the occupants in mind. In fact, being completely lined with asbestos 'fibrolite', or 'fibro' sheets, made it downright dangerous to live in (although that was not known at the time).

It was definitely a memorable experience, growing up under a corrugated iron roof. In winter, it was freezing and in the summer, it was an oven, but the most lasting memory I have is of the sound of rain and hail falling on it. Listening to torrential tropical rain pelting on an iron roof while drifting off to sleep is the most wonderfully comforting experience. The sound of the raindrops landing on metal gets louder, then softer, as the bands of rain pass over it, lulling children all tucked up under their blankets gently into slumber.

The same cannot be said of the sound of hail hitting the roof. That sounds more like an express train barrelling along overhead. Absolutely nothing can be heard except the roar of ice pellets crashing onto metal. The great advantage, however, of having a corrugated iron roof over a tiled one was that the hail stones could never break through. The bigger they were, we observed, the higher they bounced off the corrugated iron roofs across the street from us.

As soon as a hail or electrical storm broke, we three older children would rush with excitement to the open front porch to watch Mother Nature venting her fury. I loved the wild, raw energy she would unleash from the liquorice-green storm clouds ("Sky's green – hail," Mum would say), blowing the treetops sideways; lighting up the skies with blinding flashes of light and booming thunderclaps overhead which shook the very foundations of the house.

We would cram into the corner railings of our covered front porch, shouting with excitement, "See that? Woooah! Di'ja see that?" Our own mother would be cowering indoors with our baby brother, Terry, begging us to come inside for fear of lightning strikes.

Mother Nature venting her fury.

Once, the hail that fell during a storm was so big, we thought someone had thrown chunks of ice out of an old ice box onto the street outside. The hailstones were the size of tennis balls, and some even larger than that. The boy who lived across the street, B.L., picked one stone up to show us, raising it triumphantly above his head. It was almost as big as a house brick, covering the palms of both his hands!

As soon as a hailstorm passed over, we would rush outside and gather up the icy stones, throwing them at hard surfaces to make them shatter. Inside each stone was a series of concentric circles of white and clear ice rings, apparently made by the stones' rising and falling as they formed in the storm clouds.

Brisbane often finds itself sitting in the path of cyclones, and one particularly bad one hit when I was quite young. It uprooted the big willow tree next door and, when calm was restored, my dad helped the neighbour to cut up its torn branches and broken roots and remove them.

During the storm, the winds were gusting so strongly that we could feel the whole house being lifted up from its stumps. Mum rushed to the lee side of the house and flung open the windows. This, apparently, reduces upward pressure on the roof and helps prevent it from being lifted off the walls of the house and tossed away. To my recollection, we never lost any of the corrugated iron sheets which covered our roof, although many other households did, and the tiled roofs of the 1970s built houses would be shattered, or blown completely away.

As this particular cyclone passed over us and we entered into the calmness of the eye, the darkened inside of the house became suddenly very still and eerie, the air still buzzing with electric charge. The second burst of wind that passed over us seemed less violent and shorter lived than the first wave, and soon the storm dissipated and all that was left was the random plopping of stray blobs of rain on the roof. We were so fortunate that we never suffered serious damage to ourselves or our property from cyclones, although Dad's car took some serious dents from the giant hailstones.

One surprising feature of our otherwise featureless house was the window glass, which was opaque and imported all the way from Italy! It looked like bubbles all stuck together on the top of the bath. I found out it was Italian because I was hanging about when an insurance agent came to assess an insurance claim for the repair of storm damage to our home. Several panes of window glass had been broken and the household insurance was needed to replace them. Showing the insurance assessor around the house, my mother took him to see a window Greg had broken with a cricket ball. Being a child who tried to be as honest as I was pedantic, I immediately reminded Mum of this fact. The insurance assessor was very discreet and kind, assuring me that he thought my mother's version of events was the right one. The glass couldn't be matched, so we had to have unmatched window panes after that.

The effect the opaque glass windows had on the occupants of the house was that no one could ever see out of them when they were closed. In order to see outside, the windows had to be open. For this reason, except in tropical downpours or the few very coldest weeks of the winter, the windows remained open.

Having permanently open windows could prove to be a bonus at times. When our baby brother arrived, Mum would often banish Dianne, Greg and I from the house out into the yard so she could get some peace.

Having permanently open windows could prove to be a bonus.

To my brother Greg, commands were not rules to be obeyed, so much as suggestions to be accommodated (or perhaps challenges to be overcome) and on one occasion, having gone out into the yard to play, he decided he had done as he was told for long enough to demonstrate obeisance and now was free to do what he wanted. Being only 18 months apart, we were usually partners in crime, and he and I climbed up the tank stand and back into the house via his open bedroom window. When we were discovered and promptly put back outside, we went straight round the back and did it again!

The block of land our house was built on was long and narrow, about the size of two tennis courts. It was on the east side of the street, sloping down in two directions, both south and east. The front of the house faced west, towards the mountain, and our bedroom faced east, towards the rising sun, with my bed under the east-facing window. Every morning, I was treated to the glories of an Australian dawn.

Many a winter's morning I would sit on the end of my bed and watch the sun's shimmering, golden orb emerge above the treetops on the eastern horizon. Its rays tumbled out across the topmost branches of the tallest trees, touching them gold, and revealing dark undulations beneath, still out of the reach of its diffusing light. In the crisp sweetness of the morning air, the dawn chorus of native birds would herald the first sunrays of the new day.

Many, many years later, I was to discover some verses in my Bible, in the story of Job, which described my memories of those sunrises so perfectly, it gave me goose bumps when I read them. It seemed as if God Himself had been sharing those sunrises with me, long before I had heard His call on my life.

… have you commanded the morning
or assigned the dawn its place,
that it might spread to the ends of the earth …
The earth takes shape like clay under a seal;
its hills stand out like the folds of a garment.

Job 38:12-14

From the most glorious to the goriest … as mentioned previously, our house had no town water or sewerage connected, but relied on the collection of rainwater from the roof and the collection of sewerage by men who came weekly to remove and replace the cans from the outside toilet. I promised to tell more about the outside toilet, as I am sure it is of great interest.

About a third of the way down the back yard, at the end of a crumbling cement path, was the outhouse, also known as 'the dunny', 'the bog', 'the thunder box', and other names which my dad used which are too rude to mention. Sitting on a square concrete slab, it had wooden walls and a heavy, slatted wooden door which closed with a twirling wooden latch. Inside was a wooden floor, and in the centre of the back wall, what my dad would refer to as 'the throne'.

This was a cube-shaped box, also made from wood, with a lid that was fixed at the back on a hinge, similar to modern toilet seats. An oval shaped hole was cut into the top of the wooden box, the internal edges of which sloped smoothly inwards and it was surprisingly comfortable for sitting bottoms on. The lid on top was flat and solid, sealing the entire top of the box. Housewives nagging people to put the toilet seat down is nothing new. We were always being nagged to put the lid down on the toilet after use, to avoid fly infestation.

A metal pan (or can) sat inside, which could be accessed from either inside, with the twist of a wooden peg which held the front of the box in place, or outside by a trap door in the back wall. Each week, when the can was full, men from the council would come down the road with a flat-tray truck, running in an empty can and removing the full one. Popping the lid off the empty can and placing it over the full can, safely securing the contents, they would then fling it up onto their shoulders and run back up the driveway to their truck. Deftly, it would be slid along the tray to the 'full' section and another 'empty' can grabbed and hoisted over the shoulder for delivery to the next house. In pairs, they would progress down the street, one each side of the road, shouting to the driver to creep along in the truck to keep pace.

Nothing got in the way of the dunny-men, and they stopped for no one. It was not unknown to have the toilet can whipped away from underneath a bare bottom as its owner sat, legs waggling, on the seat inside. Come Christmas time, my neighbour, Auntie Grace, would always leave a shilling[22] out for the dunny-man, as it was the worst job anybody could ever think of.

There was no light in the outside toilet and no windows, only gaps under the iron roof for ventilation, nor was anything ever painted – it was all thick, raw timber. There was a large lidless wooden box next to the toilet seat which would be filled with sawdust, and a hand scoop made of a cutaway metal cylinder attached to a wooden handle and a leather strap which was used to scoop out the sawdust and sprinkle it on top of the latest deposits. This was a surprisingly effective means of containing the smell, as long as it was used faithfully. By way of a testimony to its effectiveness, in thinking about the old outhouse, what I remember most clearly was the lovely smell of fresh, yellow sawdust shavings. Waxy white toilet paper hung from a bent wire and wood hanger on the wall, and when

[22] Worth about £1.25 today.

that ran out, there was a pile of outdated newspapers that fulfilled the same function.

The walls and seats in the outhouse were not regularly cleaned, but Mum would swish the floor with a bucket of water and disinfectant – particularly if there were maggots escaping the pan and crawling around on the floor. Interestingly, it is now well known that untreated timber has antibacterial properties, both in its makeup, and by the nature of its surface, which inhibits the growth of bacteria.

Our outhouse was the home of innumerable daddy long-legs, but fortunately, unlike the famous song, we never had any red-backs under our toilet seat.

Some families were discreet about the positioning of their outhouse, but not us. Ours stood, bold as brass, right in the middle of the yard, away from everything but grass, although various attempts at decorum were made by overgrowing it with vines or decorative shrubs.

There were no native bushes or trees left on our plot, having all been cleared, and it was now mainly covered in rough, tough kikuyu grass with patches of blue couch in the front yard and on the footpath. The blue couch grew flat to the ground and spread quickly, and Mum, who prized it highly, would pull up the runners from the top of the soil and plant them all over the rest of the lawn in the hope that it would spread.

Other grasses (and even an ornamental grass – papyrus)[23] seeded themselves all over the yard and were as much weeds

[23] Papyrus is an ancient grass that was used by the Egyptians to make the first paper. Its long stalks are soft and fibrous. Dead

as any of the other weeds. Some grew thick-bladed and tough, with heavy, drooping seed heads (holcus) and some had beautifully soft and fluffy reddish pink seed heads (red natal) which we used to play tricks on unsuspecting playmates.

Gathering up a bunch of these appealing, pink grass stalks from the footpath, we would tell our victim to bite on the stems and then quickly pull the stems through their lips, stripping off the fluffy seeds as they went. They would be left spitting out the nuisance fluff and seeds from around their mouths and teeth for ages.

The worst of the weeds in our yard was a small plant which grew close to the ground with lacy fronds for leaves, like small carrot tops. It went largely undetected, unless it spread to form a big patch, as it was a brighter green than the browner winter grass in which it grew. It was called 'bindii' (bindi-eye), 'bindis' or just 'prickles'. You certainly knew if you had trodden on a patch of bindis. At its centre grew a rosette of interlocking spikes which hardened as they matured. Anybody not wearing shoes across the yard and stepping into a patch of ripe bindis would instantly experience searing pain inflicted by the unyielding, upward facing spikes. They could find a whole bunch of these nasty, little, brown prickles sticking out from the underside of their feet, like so many Lilliputian arrows and spears.

My mother told me a story once about the bindi patch in our back yard that makes me laugh out loud, even now, whenever I think of it. Dianne and Greg, being a little older than myself, had pestered her to be allowed to camp out in a disused bird aviary that had made its way from the neighbour's yard into our own (after the afore-mentioned cyclone) and been dumped there, under the willow tree. Reluctantly, Mum agreed and set them up with blankets and pillows for the night.

---

papyrus stalks were yet another plant we liked to pretend were cigarettes.

Dad arrived home later on, well after dark, and decided to play a trick on them. He took one of Mum's large white bedsheets, intending to go down the back yard in the dark, pull it over his head and start 'hoo-ing' and 'woo-ing' like a ghost, to give them both a good fright. Minus his shoes, Dad began tiptoeing down the yard, holding the sheet up over his head.

Suddenly, landing a bare foot in the bindi patch in the middle of the yard, he let out a yelp of pain and, throwing the sheet aside, started jumping up and down in the dark, pulling the prickles out of one foot while trying not to stand in any more with the other.

Dad arrived home later on, well after dark, and decided to play a trick on them.

My siblings, recognising his voice, stuck their heads out of the old aviary and fell about laughing at him. The story made Mum laugh with the telling, so I guess she was watching the fiasco out of the kitchen window.

My mother spent a lot of time looking out of the kitchen window – probably because she spent a lot of time in the kitchen. Before the town water was connected, the side entrance to our house had faced down the back, with steps going down to a path leading to the outhouse, or turning left to go to the tank, or then on to the area under the house that accommodated the washing machine.

Mum's washing machine was a manual top-loader with a central agitator and an enormous and very dangerous mangle. Mum would feed clothes into the agitating blades of the machine, then pull out the wet washing and feed it through the mangle, which would squeeze it flat, returning the soapy water back to the machine and sending the clothes on into a deep cement tri-partite trough for rinsing. When she did a 'whites' wash, she would put a little bag of blue dye in with the rinse water to make the clothes brighter. Sometimes, she would put starch flakes in with Dad's shirts, as well. I can smell the warm, sudsy water as I write. They would then be fed back through the mangle (set to reverse) and held up to be directed into a clothes basket, ready to take them down to the clothesline.

When the water tank went, and the outhouse went, the original washing line also went, to be replaced by the new, immensely popular, aluminium 'Hill's Hoist'. While Mum wanted it to hang clothes on, we children were more interested in using it as a merry-go-round. Mum (and every other mother in the land) could regularly be heard shouting, "You kids, stop swinging on the line!"

The floor level of the house at the back was just high enough for an adult to stand upright underneath it, but it rapidly decreased towards the front of the house, so some of the slope underneath the house had been cut away and cement retaining walls laid in. The greater part of 'under the house' had thus been made into a useful working and storage space.

It saw little of any type of work, although Dad did have a greasy woodwork bench, complete with a massive, clunking iron vice attached, which I used to enjoy playing with (well, squashing my fingers in). However, there was certainly a generous amount of storage: tools, tins of nuts and bolts, building materials of various sorts, more old farming equipment, bricks, paint and paint brushes and glass jars full of turpentine in which paintbrushes had been left to soak, now captured in a solidified skin of paint, like tall ships in an Arctic ice floe. There were pieces of wood, birdcages, car parts, more car parts, rusty saws and broken sieves, picks, a metal trunk of army rations[24] and wooden trunks with nothing in, and a clothes line strung from one end to the other in case of rainy days. And where did we get a pair of ancient, hand-operated sheep shears? … or a boot-maker's anvil?? In theory, this assortment of junk should all have long since made its way 'down the back'.

I'm not sure why there were so many paint pots under the house – not much painting got done! Dad painted the hallway once – a fluorescent pink colour – for which Mum's only explanation was that he was colour blind. This couldn't have been true, as he was in the army. Although she did tell me a funny story about Dad and his painting…

Our roof, being made of corrugated iron, needed the odd coat of silver coloured paint. This helped to stop any rust from forming, but also helped to reflect some of the sun's heat. Dad

[24]Our father had been on his way to Vietnam and had brought home a metal trunk of army rations suitable for the jungle. He never went to Vietnam, but we raided the trunk, ate the disgusting chocolate, made tents out of the khaki blankets, ran around the yard in his tin helmet, and chopped down vegetation with the machete. Who lets children play with a machete?

took it upon himself to do this 'simple' job. Having climbed onto the roof with all his equipment, he decided the best plan of action was to start from the guttering and work his way up. Finishing the lowest level, he put a foot out behind to push himself upward and accidentally stepped into the wet paint.

His foot shot out from beneath him and he followed, front down, all the way down the roof, paintbrush in hand, until he went over the guttering and right off the edge. Fortunately, he managed to grab the gutter for a moment and broke his fall, so he was unharmed, but his arms, face and the front of his overall were completely covered in silver paint. Mum found this very funny indeed, as my father's nickname was 'Silver' because his hair had turned grey at a very young age.

Amongst the cast-offs under the house was a wobbly, blunt pair of hair-cutting scissors – black metal and very long and pointy – which I used to cut the ribbon ties right off my pretty, frilly bonnet (page 161). They had somehow made their way downstairs from upstairs, where they had been the only pair of scissors in the house. Perhaps I had sneaked them down.

I cut one side because the ribbon had frayed at the end, then it was uneven, so I cut the other side … and so it went on … Those scissors also provided me with some very dubious haircuts.

The very cramped area under the front porch offered just enough space for me to crawl into and sit in, so I went about making myself a secret place there for hiding all sorts of treasures, lining them up along the fence railings that screened off the underneath of the house, as if in a museum. I had a selection of pretty and interestingly shaped rocks, a few shells, a sea urchin skeleton and goodness knows what else.

My best exhibit was a rectangular metal box with a hinged lid which I had found discarded between my lichen fence and the garage next door, amongst a load of scrap wood, fencing wire and fibro. When I first opened it, it still contained the remnants of some velvety, purple fabric which disintegrated as I pulled it out. I believe it once was an ink box for stamping official papers. The lid had become very slightly bent, so it was offset, and would not close properly. Perhaps that was why it had been thrown away – the ink pad in it would have dried out.

Greg and I would sometimes sit under the front porch and wait for Mum to toss lit cigarette butts out of the front door and into the garden bed next to us, then, reaching through where a paling was missing from the fence, we would retrieve the butt end and finish smoking it. Greg and I were always trying to smoke something!

Perhaps Mum was always by the kitchen windows because she was always throwing things out of them. In those days, all our food was fresh and chickens came from the butcher, gutted and beheaded, but with legs and feet still attached, since it was by the feet they were trussed and hung in the butcher's window.

In preparing a chicken to roast, Mum would first have to take her big carving knife and wallop off the legs of the chicken at the knees. These chicken feet, complete with claws, would be tossed out of the kitchen window and land on the grass near to the rubbish bin.[25] My brother and I would pounce on the amputated limbs, pulling at the exposed white tendons to make the claws open and close, then chase one another around the yard, pretending the feet were still alive.

---

[25] Because of the problem with flies, there were no bins kept inside the house, only a large metal one outside.

Other things that got disposed of via the open kitchen window were empty bottles, cans, vegetable peelings, fish guts and crab shells wrapped up in newspaper, ice from defrosting the freezer, and pots of soggy white spaghetti that had sat all night on the stove. Eventually it all made it into the bin. I think Mum's pressure cooker sat outside 'on the cement' for a good few years. 'On the cement' was a very useful place – it was used to sharpen the carving knife, split open pumpkins and watermelons, and served as a solid base on which to smash open the thick woody shells of macadamia nuts (Bauple nuts to us) with a hammer or half a brick.

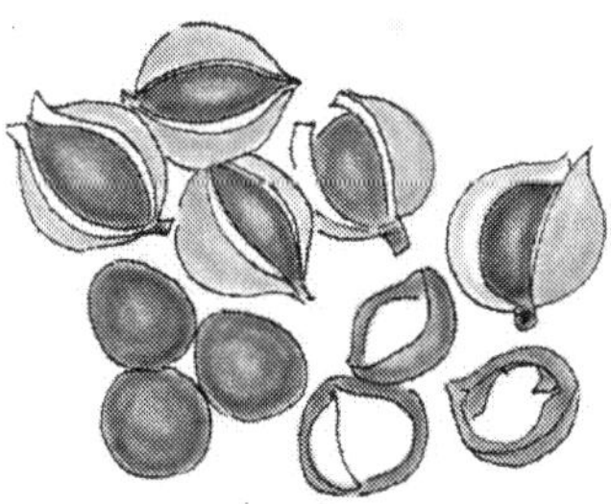

The best source of Bauple nuts for miles around was on Creek Road, in the yard of the house next to Howatson's bus shed, as mentioned earlier. The tree grew right on the boundary between that property and Howatson's dilapidated bus shed next door.

The 'nut tree' was always surrounded by children picking up the nuts that had fallen in their split green and brown casings, much in the same way that British children collect conkers wrapped up in outer casings from underneath horse chestnut trees. Inside the thin outer shell was a hard wooden nut, also similar in colour to conkers, a rich reddish/brown, and it needed a perfectly timed and weighted blow from a very hard object in order to split it open to reveal its creamy, rich contents. Too soft, and the nut would bounce up and strike a painful blow on the face, too hard, and the shell would shatter into the kernel, ruining it completely with nasty, hard wooden shards. I don't know who owned the yard that the tree grew in – I suspect the church next door – but nobody ever objected to the crowd of nut scavengers under their tree when the nuts ripened and fell. The nut tree, sadly, met its demise when a block of flats was eventually built on the site of the old house.

Our kitchen was quite poorly equipped by modern standards, consisting of a small fridge with an inbuilt freezer section, a stove, a sink and two wall cupboards – the sort that had sliding glass doors and sloped from a wide top to a narrow bottom – which were painted burnt orange inside. They were quite useless as anything much more than display cases. Mum kept her few nice pieces of bone china and decorative plates in one of them and her every day mismatched crockery and glassware in the other.

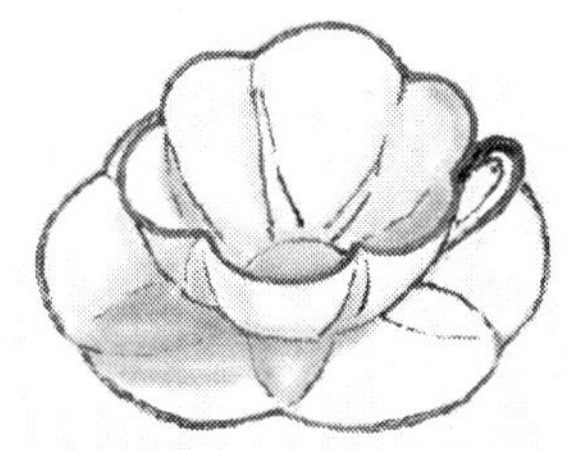

In a curious way, the contents of our house mirrored the position Australia held on the world stage at that time – holding on to the Mother Country, Britain, while reaching out to embrace Asia and the Orient. This pre-emptive fusion of East and West was evident in Mum's kitchen cabinets and also came as a legacy of our father's time spent in Japan after the war (page 164). On one side was displayed her finest bone china teacup and saucer by Shelley and some majolica plates from England with their anemones and foxgloves, and on the other was the mixed up remains of a fashionable Japanese Noritake dinner service and Midwinter crockery, also from the UK.

In the centre of the room, and mostly filling it, was a dining table and chairs. When my younger brother Terry arrived, a wooden highchair was added to the mix. When he outgrew his highchair, an even bigger dining table with six chairs was somehow squeezed into the space.

A red aluminium teapot, faded to dark pink, with a raised motif around the top, sat in the centre of the table, along with two long, funnel-shaped salt and pepper shakers. Like the three pillars of sustainability, these permanent features were used to prop up Dad's newspaper. He always read at the kitchen table (while he ate his dinner and watched telly). In fact, he was always reading, everywhere – in the kitchen, in bed, in the toilet...

The salt shaker had dry rice grains added, to help push the salt out when the summer humidity had made it so wet, it no longer flowed. Alongside the teapot sat a sugar bowl with a lid on it. Otherwise, being vaguely under the ceiling light, visitors risked having a few bits of moth's wing along with the two spoons of sugar in their tea. A heavy, square, glass ashtray was always on the table and usually full of stale cigarette butts and ash. Smoking was not known to be so dangerous back in those days.

In one awkward corner of the kitchen, next to the stove, there was a wireless radio, a breadbin and a toaster. The toaster was the type that needed to be monitored at all times, having a central element and two trays on springs that would be pulled back to check the progress of the toasting. Turn away for one moment and the toast would be burnt.

My mother may not have had much in the way of kitchen facilities, but she always provided freshly cooked, well balanced, nutritious meals (three colours of vegetables, a portion of carbs and a portion of protein), and we only had pudding (tinned fruit, or jelly and ice cream) on a Sunday evening after a roast dinner. Spices of any sort were forbidden by my father – particularly garlic. However, Mum did boil sausages in my dad's beer.

In those days, processed foods were limited to what was desiccated and packaged (like powdered soup) or tinned (like tinned soup) and the latest fashion in adventurous cooking was to make meals entirely from recipes on the backs of tinned and dried ingredients. Mum's salmon casserole was amazingly good, but the ingredients were a bit bizarre.[26]

No one ever drained the fat off anything, or grilled it off, and the same cast iron pan would be used time and again to fry bacon, sausages, chops or steak. The fat which rendered out of the meat was left to solidify and then scraped off before the next use. The fat from roast beef was passed through a sieve into a special enamel pot and kept in the fridge. Called 'dripping', it was used to make fried bread, or to fry everything, really, since the idea of cooking with oil had not taken off in our house.

The browning from the roast joint was used to make gravy by adding only plain flour, salt and pepper, but I have never tasted gravy like it! It was thick and flavoursome – and the same consistency, whatever the type of meat. Whatever Mum may have lacked in the art of haute cuisine, she more than made up for with a Sunday roast and toasted cheese sandwiches (chewing gum sandwiches). She worked her magic with little more than a carving knife, a vegetable knife and a fork with which to mash boiled vegetables.

Dad, actually, was a great cook, although he never did, unless he had no choice. I remember one of his pot roasts being the best I had ever eaten,[27] although he once brought rabbit stew

---

[26] Salmon casserole: 1 large tin salmon, 1 tin cream of asparagus soup, 1 tin evaporated milk, 2 cups of cooked white rice, 1 diced onion, 1 heaped cup of grated strong cheddar, lemon juice, parsley, salt and pepper to taste. Mix in a casserole dish, sprinkle crushed cornflakes and a few knobs of butter on top, bake for 45 minutes.

[27] A pot roast is a roast dinner cooked on top of the stove in a big pot with a secure lid on it. The meat joint, usually topside of beef, is browned all over and put in first with some liquid, the lid sealed, and cooked very slowly on top of the stove. The veg is added to the juices later. All the flavours go into the juices so the gravy from them

back from a hunting trip he had gone on with some mates and that didn't go down very well. He brought back an orphaned joey at the same time, but sadly, it was too young to survive.

Dad only went on hunting trips as the cook. He wasn't a great shot. Mum was a crack shot with a hunting rifle – if she was hunting tin cans lined up down the back yard. She once sat at the boys' bedroom window to watch a high profile celebrity wedding being conducted in a church across the valley, using the sight on the barrel of my brother's hunting rifle like a pair of binoculars. "Oh, look," she observed, "there's security guards everywhere. I wonder why." Probably looking for snipers with rifles in bedroom windows.

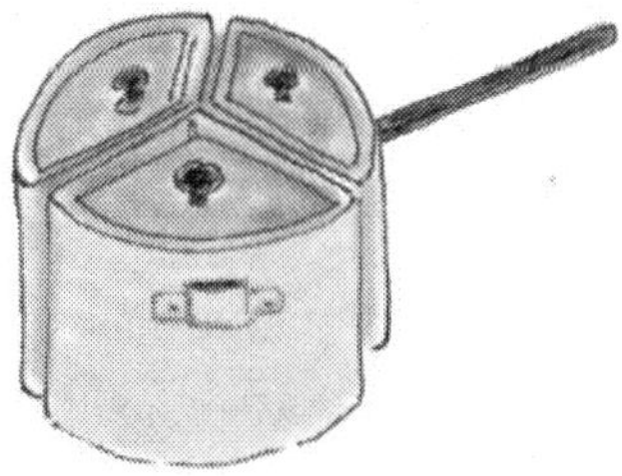

Mum had a set of three saucepans that fitted together on one electric ring of the stove, each having a triangular lid, but sharing one Bakelite handle. This nifty design allowed her to cook three vegetables on one electric ring. I spent many hours on the kitchen floor spinning those lids like tops.

A hallway led out of the kitchen and straight down into the bathroom, with three bedrooms coming off to the sides. The bathroom contained only a deep enamel bathtub, a sink with a small mirrored cabinet above, and a corner cupboard, which housed several sets of encyclopaedia, for want of any more suitable storage space. I spent many, many hours poring over those encyclopaedia and their sepia images of the wonders of the world, such as Stonehenge, never dreaming that one day I would stand in the footprints of the photographer, mesmerised by the mysterious, ancient monoliths.

---

is wonderfully rich.

Our bedrooms were small, but we had so few possessions to store in them, and we spent so much time outdoors, we didn't really notice when we were very young. Dianne and I shared a wardrobe and a dresser, called 'the duchess', which had originally belonged to Mum and one of her many sisters (she had five sisters and three brothers). It had three tiers. One was a small cupboard with a pull out tray and there were three drawers, two on one level and one on the next, so it went down in stages. The suite had lovely turned wood Queen Anne legs. The boys' room was so small that once there were two beds, a grey wardrobe and a tiny grey dresser squeezed into it, the door couldn't even be closed!

The lounge room was the largest room in the house and had part-glazed hardwood double doors which opened onto the front porch. In the centre of the room was a huge, glass-topped dining table that had belonged to my grandmother, a black and white television on spindly legs in one corner, and a very uncomfortable bumpy vinyl sofa and two matching chairs with highly-polished wooden arms lined the other walls.

The television could not be seen from the sofa for the dining table, so we usually lay on the lovingly waxed and polished hardwood floor (the only other bit of 'special' in the house design) to watch telly – what little of it there was to watch. There were only three terrestrial channels at first, then I remember another one coming along. There was no remote control. If the television needed to be turned off, or the channel changed, someone had to get up, walk across the room and turn the knob.

Although there was not much to be watched on television, we used to have an outmoded radiogram, which was housed in a polished wooden cabinet and consisted of both a radio and a record player. The record player played '78' records, which spun around really quickly. My favourite record was the soundtrack from the musical 'Annie Get Your Gun' with Doris Day.

Dad, who loved to dance, would put our feet on his feet and dance along to the music, whisking us around the polished wood floor until we were so giddy, we slipped off his feet and fell in a giggling heap on the floor. That was, of course, when he wasn't torturing us by flipping our feet into the backs of our pyjama bottoms and laughing riotously as we struggled, spinning around in circles on our stomachs, trying to get them out again.

My siblings and I used to play a game together when we had to turn the television off to go to bed. The picture would reduce down to a small dot in the centre of the screen when the 'off' button was pressed (with its huge 'ker-chunk') and it would remain there for a few seconds before fading completely. The game was to cover the dot with a hand and then guess when it had disappeared (no peeking allowed). This was accompanied by the chanting of, "When I say the dot is gone, the dot…is…gone!"

Television programs ceased well before midnight and, should we be up that late for some reason, we would stand to hear 'God Save the Queen' being played before broadcasting shut down for the night.

We didn't have a telephone. In those days, if some urgent information needed to be conveyed, the local police would be dispatched with a message, or a telegram sent, which would be delivered by someone from the post office. We were on the receiving end of both those services over the course of the years – when relatives hundreds of miles away had passed away. There was a moment of heightened anxiety the day the police called at the door to notify my father of a death in his family. I think someone may have had a guilty conscience!

The most valuable items in the lounge lived in a small round-shouldered cabinet that sat under the side window. It was Mum's collection of crystal pieces that she had begun when she worked at Tritton's department store in Queen Street, in the city, before she married. They only came out at Christmas – and then only the trifle bowls, in which she would make a very potent sherry trifle. They still come out at Christmas for sherry trifle now, in the UK.

Apart from that, these twinkling plates, bowls, glasses and vases would come out once every so often to be washed in washing powder and vinegar, then air-dried and lovingly replaced behind their sliding glass doors. My mum showed me how to test the quality of the crystal by pinging it with my fingernail and listening to the pitch and duration of the ring. The higher the pitch, the higher the lead content, and the better the quality and sparkle of the piece.

Other articles of interest in our home were various pieces which had been sent home from Japan by our father, who had been in the British Commonwealth Occupational Forces after

the war. There were silk table runners, a silk sheet embroidered with dragons, table cloths and matching napkins; a delicate silk painting of a geisha; a mother-of-pearl sailing ship carved out of a single, enormous clam shell; various black lacquer photo albums inlaid with mother-of-pearl, and jewellery boxes depicting typical Japanese scenes, like Fujiyama and cherry blossom.

We were the only children in our neighbourhood who knew that 'Fujiyama' meant 'Mount Fuji', so it was incorrect to say, 'Mt Fujiyama'. We knew no one else who ate seaweed biscuits, and once, when Dad said he nearly shipped home a dishwasher, I had visions of a little Japanese slave person in apron and rubber gloves, tied to the kitchen sink. In our already overcrowded little house, I wondered where they were going to sleep.

When town water was connected, the outhouse could no longer be used and my parents had to provide a place for a new flush toilet to be installed. They did so by turning the side porch around to face the front and adding an extension to the side of the kitchen at the back. We spent the rest of our years at home opening the front door and looking straight into the toilet, then turning into the kitchen and looking straight down the hall into the bathroom.

The loss of the back steps also brought about the unexpected loss of many of the familiar routines we had developed as a family. Dad used to sit on the back steps in the winter sunshine and polish the brass buckles on his webbed belts with Brasso (since he was still a soldier).

Once, when he was required to march in a military parade at the barracks in Bulimba where he was stationed, he spent ages sitting on the back steps, spit polishing his parade boots and rubbing his brass uniform fittings, including his 'Rising Sun' badge for his slouch hat, with a soft cloth, eradicating even the merest hint of a fingerprint. He showed me how to spit polish, but I wasn't allowed to help. Nobody, not even Mum, was allowed to polish Dad's uniform brass or his boots. One of my very first memories was of seeing Dad coming home one night in his khaki uniform and not being sure who he was, since I usually only saw him on the weekends when he wasn't wearing his uniform.

The back steps were the place where we sat in the sunshine, brushing our hair dry after it had been washed. Dianne, Greg and I would sit, each on a different step, every night before bed, waiting in turn to traipse down the path for the day's last visit to the outside toilet. Terry would have been too young still, so would have had a potty inside the house. Mum would sweep the dust and crumbs out of the house with her straw broom onto the back steps, flicking them backwards under the porch, as if that made them go away. Neighbours visited and small bottles of beer (called 'stubbies') were shared on the back steps.

There was a certain level of privacy, even intimacy, which sitting on the back steps afforded us that the front steps, in full view of the passing traffic on the street, just didn't. When the inside toilet was added to the side of the kitchen, the new stairs, now facing the front of the house, were fewer, too shallow to sit on comfortably, and too public, as the side door then became the most used entrance to the house.

A delicate silk painting of a geisha.

Chapter 8

The Creek

In writing about the creek at the end of my stories, I am definitely leaving the best until last. The creek ran parallel with the main road at the bottom of our street. Despite my best efforts, I have never discovered its name (if you discount the names I gave it myself when I was busy being David Livingstone). I think it was just known as Bulimba Creek, being one of the many tributaries that flowed into that creek.

The creek was like an extension to my own yard. I spent endless hours there, traversing pathways made by others in the long grass, and making pathways myself. The constant trickling of water over stones was very soothing and the hours that would be spent down at the creek flew away like minutes. I only had to be home in time for tea, so it was fortunate that I could tell the time by the length of the shadows and the temperature of the air.

There was a sense of resilience, of permanence, about the creek (or 'the gully', as it was also known), even though its actual features were constantly changing. There was a sort of assumption I had made that it had always been there and would always be there. Even when its clay banks had been twisted and contorted by torrents of summer storm water, it would return quickly to its level and simply carry on, its features only slightly altered.

The very first memories I have of the creek was a single occasion when Auntie Grace, who must have been looking after me for my mum, took me over to her friend's house, which could be seen across the valley from the high vantage point on Auntie Grace's back porch. It had a red brick frontage and looked back at us from the ridge on the other side of the creek. There was nothing in between Creek Road and her friend's house in Rothwell Street except the houses on our side, the main road, the creek itself, and a lot of long grass with a vague sort of path trodden through it.

Local people ... would replace them with more dubiously bouncy wooden planks.

The creek had not yet been channelled underground from Chrysler Street to Fairland Street and the ground it ran through was open, and undeveloped. Huge underground storm pipes would soon be laid through which to direct the water's flow underground, and the land would be cleared for house building along the newly laid Chrysler, Dykes, Exchange and Dalgety Streets.

Walking together down the hill, Auntie Grace and I crossed Creek Road and the creek, although I cannot remember what the crossing looked like. There may even have been the beginnings of a proper road at this point, but there were no houses or streets along this strip of land at this time. A lower dirt road, which ran in tandem with the main road from Fairland Street to somewhere opposite Raffles Street, gave access to the driveways of the houses built along the south side of Creek Road. It was to become the lower level of Creek Road along this stretch when it was sealed and concrete retaining walls put between the two levels in the 1970s. A most magnificent gum that grew on the footpath opposite Howatson's bus shelter was sacrificed to the upgrade of Creek Road to dual carriageway along this stretch.

The 'bridges' over the creek were not so much bridges, as a couple of planks someone put down so people could cross the gully without having to take the very long way around via the existing roads. There were five crossings along the section of creek from Bothwell Street to Newnham Road. The first was in the field at the end of Bothwell Street and the next between two houses on Creek Road, joining up to the bend where Vulcan and Marlene Streets meet. There was a crossing of some description where Chrysler Street now is, a wooden bridge at Fairland Street, and another one down near Mt Gravatt East State School, which I don't remember personally. These makeshift crossings would easily be washed away when the creek flooded after severe rainfall. Local people, wanting the convenience of crossing points, would replace them with more dubiously bouncy wooden planks.[28]

As I trudged along beside Auntie Grace towards her friend, Mrs. H.'s house, I vividly remember looking up the grassy slope and thinking what a long way there was to go. I was quite quickly beginning to regret coming! And I remember Auntie Grace accommodating my little legs by sitting me for a few moments on a big old log lying in the rough grass by the side of the path, before resuming our walk up the hill. Even

---

[28] In later years, a school friend taking one of these shortcuts home late at night after a lot of rain, prudently turned back from the bridge crossing as he thought the water in the creek sounded strange. He took the long way home instead. It was a good decision. The creek had swollen, broken its banks and washed the bridge away, but he was unable to see it in the darkness.

though sitting down for a bit sounded like a good idea, my relief at being allowed to rest was tempered by my anxiety that there may be snakes in the decaying trunk, as that was the standard warning given to children about hollow, fallen logs.

The first of the wooden crossing bridges was behind the BCC supermarket on Logan Road. The creek must have come out of an underground culvert somewhere near the bottom of Bothwell Street (which had ended at the footpath between Walton's and a house with a magnificent lantana hedge). By the time it reached the spot where the steps are now cut into the low retaining wall on the extended stretch of Bothwell Street, it was wide and shallow enough for children to stop on their way home from school and play in the water.

He had taken them off to play in the water.

The creek was bridged at this point so mums and children could take a shortcut across the open field to the back of the shops and the footpath leading up to the main shopping area at the terminus, without having to go the long way around via the Logan Road junction.

Before Terry was born, Mum and I would sometimes walk up to the school in the afternoon to collect Dianne and Greg when they came down the sweeping front drive to the school gates. But generally, both Dianne and Greg were left to make their own way home after school. The temptation to stop at the bridge and play in the cool water of the creek was often too much for Greg to resist. Mum had to walk all the way back down to the creek crossing to find Greg's shoes on more than one occasion, and once for only one of Greg's shoes. "Brand new desert boots!" she went out of the door, cursing under her breath. He had taken them off to play in the water and only one had made it home.

From Bothwell Street, the creek flowed through the empty field towards Creek Road, was channelled under the road and came out the other side, running roughly parallel to Creek Road, behind a single row of houses, and from there, down to the convergence of Creek, Wecker and Newnham Roads. Flowing around the back of what was Wilkinson's sawmill and a car breaker's yard, it continued on to an old tannery which was positioned on its south bank, surrounded by bush, just before joining the main flow of Bulimba Creek. The remains of now-empty farm paddocks could still be found down at this end of Mt Gravatt, with the occasional horse or horse trough and rickety timber-slatted and wire fence.

This mile-and-a-half stretch[29] of creek was ours to explore and play in, and the older we got, the further afield we went. We would run up and down inside the storm pipes, shouting as loudly as possible and so the echo went on as long as we could make it last. Over the years, further sections of the creek would be diverted underground to make way for roads, houses, and industrial areas. Now, only the section from Fairfield Street onwards remains above ground, at first channelled, and

---

[29] Equal to about 2.7 kilometres.

then reverting to its natural state, on and off, through various recreation areas, until it reaches Bulimba Creek.

My introduction to exploring the creek was made by a friend, A.M., who lived in one of the houses on the lower side of Creek Road, at the bottom of our street. Their side and back fences formed part of the boundary to the thick, scrubby bushland through which the creek flowed, so they were very familiar with its secret paths and hiding places. My friend's brother once produced a legless lizard from the side wall and chased us around with great glee as we screamed our heads off, before it occurred to me that he wouldn't be doing that if it was a poisonous snake.

The reward for my efforts was a handful of delicate pink peach blossom.

It was from their house that I plucked up the courage to fight my way through the long grass and bracken to reach a ragged old peach tree which was in full spring bloom. The reward for my efforts was a handful of delicate pink peach blossom to take home to my mum. I was pretty-well hooked after this: my first bush expedition.

Golden wattle also grew by the peach tree, and, oblivious to the cuts and scratches inflicted in the process, I would gather great armfuls of it when it flowered in the spring and bring it home up the hill. The warm honey scent of the golden balls of blossom would fill my nostrils and I would breathe it in as deeply as I could. Glorious as the fresh wattle bloom was, by the next day, it would simply have shrivelled up and gone brown – its potent aroma turned to something dead and decaying. I did eventually learn just to enjoy it on the bough.

The first section of the creek, from Bothwell Street to where it crossed Creek Road, was diverted underground so that the New World Shopping Centre could be built on the site.

Coles New World Shopping Centre was a bit of a revolution in shopping. It was a grocery store, all under one roof, but there were other independent traders alongside it. Amongst them was a butcher, a chemist, a gift shop and hairdresser, a laundromat, a café where Mum worked when we were older, and a Chinese takeaway. The family who had the Chinese takeaway had a son the same age as our brother, Terry, and even Mum used to mistake them at times when they were young.

After that, the first point of entrance to the creek was on the south side of Creek Road. It was along this stretch that penny tortoises could be found and captured, as well as the biggest bearded dragons. The banks of the creek could be quite steep and slippery – being predominantly clay. Its thick, matted and serrated-edged grasses were virtually impenetrable, but the biggest deterrent to accessing the creek in this place was the boys who lived next to it. They were quite feisty and considered this particular stretch behind their house to be their territory. It was a brave child who thought otherwise.

Not having the courage to venture up that far, my interests at first lay in the section of creek between the bridge crossing from Creek Road to Marlene Street and the storm drains which took it under Chrysler Street. It was not accessible at many points along this stretch, but we grew up liking a challenge, so no amount of personal injury put us off clambering over the rocks and fallen trees to get down to the water and see what we could see.

Where it...dropped down a small weir, we named it 'Something Falls'.

Inspired by the adventures of David Livingstone, who was a bit of a hero of mine, a good exploring buddy and I followed the course of the creek along this section, naming all its features.

Where it was joined by water pipes from under Marlene Street and dropped down a small weir made of the craggy, pitted red rocks through which the creek burbled and foamed, we named it 'Something Falls'. Where a recently collapsed bank had filled the creek bed with soil and created a shallow pool with steep, raw, banks, we named it 'Someone or Other Bay'. We put rocks in the creek to make dams and then gave the dams names. We named every rocky protrusion, every gorge and every giant gum tree we deemed noteworthy, working our way along either in the water, or where the water was too deep, along the banks beside it.[30]

In the midst of quite harsh, tangled and overgrown scrubland, there could be found some surprisingly delicate plants and flowers. The most delicate of all was the native maidenhair fern which would peep out of crevices in rock faces where they clung precariously to the sheer banks of the creek.

Right in the middle of our stretch of creek was the remaining trunk of a fallen gum tree which crossed from one bank to the other. It was quite a challenge to shuffle all the way over it, as it wasn't very wide, and it bounced precariously under our weight, as if reluctant to be made use of in such a manner. But it offered us an easier access route to the south side of the creek where the strip of remaining scrub was deeper, but more open, with less of the tangled grass and broad fronds of bracken fern that choked the north bank.

Others who had gone before us had made cubby houses (dens) under clumps of scrub by crawling into the centre where three or four bushes grew together, pulling out dead branches and levelling off the bare dirt. These scrubby bush houses could hide giggling children surprisingly well from any foreign

[30] Imagine my delight at finding myself living in a small market town in the UK where a blue plaque marked the room David Livingstone lived in before he went to Africa.

parties making their way along the narrow, trodden-down grass paths.

The long, dry grass which bordered both creek banks once ignited into a huge bushfire, threatening the safety of the houses along Creek Road and some newly built brick houses in Chrysler Street. Furiously it blazed, crackling and spitting wildly, drawing spectators from as far away as its smoke and embers travelled to watch in awe from a spare piece of ground above the entrance to the underground storm pipes. The explosive cracking of eucalyptus leaves flung golden glowing sparks far up into the sky, which then showered back down on us, covering us with spots of greasy soot. The noise was terrific.

Eventually fire engines arrived and the fire crews shooed us away as they dealt with the blaze. When it was all over, and there was nothing but blackened earth, charred branches and little wisps of smoke rising up from the very last remains of the conflagration, all the dry, matted vegetation had been cleared and the bare ground was completely exposed. Much of the mystery and promise of adventure of the creek was lost that day.

Another memorable episode was the day some boys came running up our street in a great state of excitement to tell us there was a man with a wooden leg asleep in the long grass by one of the fences down at the creek. Everyone rushed down to have a look. I caught a brief glimpse of someone lying in grass, but I wasn't about to hang around to see if he had a wooden leg! I ran back home – very quickly.

Becoming masters of our stretch of creek, we soon moved further along to see what other gangs of children were enjoying further down Creek Road. The creek was easily accessed at Fairland Street where the pipes delivered its underground flow back out into the fresh air. At this point, sand and gravel had built up at the pipes' mouths and the waterway was shallow and wide, crystal clear and sparkling as it skipped over gravel and stones on the sandbank. Lots of pond life could be seen here, such as pond skaters and vivid blue and green dragon flies which flitted about among the long grass. Fantailed guppies were abundant in the water that ran a little deeper under the grass overhanging the bank.

A gang of local children could regularly be found down in the creek with big pickle jars full of creek water, and wire coat hangers, bent into a diamond shape and covered with a discarded stocking, which they used as nets to catch fish.

Rainbow-coloured fantails were quite a prize to be taking home.

The equipment was made in a moment and the technique was simple.[31] Keeping your shadow away from the fish, so as not to alarm them or alert them to your presence, the net would be

---

[31] I remember rummaging through my mother's clothes drawers for stockings to use. I wonder now if she ever wondered then where her stockings kept disappearing to!

slipped carefully into the water under the overhanging grass and then lifted slowly up, back out of the water again.

Without fail, the wriggling bodies of several little transparent silvery fish would be left flipping around in the middle of the stocking net. They would be dropped into the pickle jar to be taken home. The plain ones, which were the females, may have been released back into the water, but the males with frilly rainbow-coloured fantails were quite a prize to be taking home. No child would leave the creek disappointed.

The meeting place at 'the bridge' in Fairland Street was also used for such tribal activities as negotiations with delegates from neighbouring territories and trading tokens of goodwill, like marbles, or just as often, ill will, like insults! When we were older – teenagers – we would sit in the sunshine on the warm wooden planks after school, smoking cigarettes and drinking Coke, well out of mothers' sightlines. I had, by this time, given up any desire to smoke anything, but it was still a good place to sit and talk with friends and wave bare legs over the side of the bridge in the remains of the summer sunshine.

Always seeking adventure, we pushed our way further along the creek bank, through swathes of matted tussock grass, around a sweeping bend, until we reached the area behind the Greek Orthodox Church. There, lying on its side in the long grass, was an enormous, dead gum tree which lay where it had fallen many years before, its top side branches jutting quite high up into the air. It was known to the local children as 'the ten headed dragon', although I think I could only count seven 'heads'. Perhaps some of its heads had fallen off over the years.

Children would come a long way to climb along the dragon's trunk and up its protruding branches to bounce them up and down. It was a rather perilous pastime, as the tree was quite rotten and the branches ready to snap. It was a long way to the ground below, but at least there was a thick mat of trampled-down long grass to cushion the fall a little.

It was known to the local children as 'the ten headed dragon'.

As much as the new, sprawling residential areas were given priority over the natural watercourses, sometimes, even the construction industry had to make compromises. When the Housing Commission built the estate which runs along the opposite side of this section of Creek Road, one spare block on the corner of Canterbury and Kentish Streets was left bare.

The reason for this anomaly in the endless rows of uniform wooden boxes under construction was that, when there had been an abundance of rain, a natural spring would surface in the middle of this block of land. Having nowhere to go, it would simply sit and make the ground boggy until the water level dropped again.

I investigated this phenomenon quite rigorously myself, poking around in the grass to try to pinpoint the exact fissure through which the water was rising from the ground beneath. In the end I simply had to be satisfied that it was somewhere there, under the sodden grass. As a consequence, no house could be built on that block of land and it remains so today. It was left as open ground and when we were young some play equipment was installed on it.

Passing the dragon's lair, the creek bed bottomed out and widened, as it approached Newnham Road. With a good mix of sand and gravel, and low banks, it provided an excellent stretch of water in which to paddle and wash the dust off tired feet. Nothing could ever be guaranteed though, as the water from heavy rains could wash away these shallows and cut new paths through the creek banks, stealing away these natural playgrounds overnight.

Further along the creek, the last place of interest that I would visit was the old tannery. The tannery had been there since the previous century, but I believe it was still in operation. It was a bit of a curiosity as a working site and I suspect at one time it must have relied on running water from the creek to put hides through the tanning process.

There was a rough bit of path through thick bushes that went down the side fence of the tannery enabling access to a wide, calm, swimming hole surrounded by scrubby bush. It was shallow enough to stand up in, but also deep enough to have a good splash about. Before anyone went into one of these swimming holes, a rock would be thrown in to chase any snakes out of the water.

In all the time I spent in the bush along the creek and up the mountain, I never saw a snake of any description, although I do think I owe thanks for avoiding one to a faithful dog, Smoky, who was owned by Auntie Grace and who accompanied us everywhere we went. Although he belonged next door, we had children in our house, so he spent most of his time in and around our house and yard, or accompanying Mum on her daily shopping trips. He lay in one spot at the top of our hallway, by the kitchen, where the wall turned almost black from a thick build-up of grease from his hair.

Smoky, who had been a stray, had two serious issues with life. No one could get him into a car (if someone offered Mum and I a lift home from the terminus, the dog would race along beside the car, turning up our street and into the yard just as we were getting out of the car and thanking the kind driver). His other great terror was of water. No one could wash him. But he was the most loyal companion a child could ever wish for. Wherever we were, there was Smoky.

One day, wandering back from the terminus with Smoky darting about, back and forth, sniffing things in general, I was alerted to something in a hole by the side of the footpath by the dog frantically barking and growling. Suddenly Smoky let out a yelp and ran to me, limping and holding up one of his front paws. There, on his paw, were two puncture wounds, just beginning to ooze blood. Smoky suffered no ill effects, so whatever had bitten him had not injected venom, but I was quite shaken when I realised he must have gone after a snake.

The creek at the bottom of our street was bulldozed over many years ago, but the memories of time spent there are as fresh as if it was yesterday. As the 1960s rolled over into the 1970s, the land on the creek's south bank was cleared for building. Skeletal house frames began sprouting up out of the bare earth where the wattle and peach blossom had previously bloomed.

My first piece of published writing was a child's lament of the loss of this strip of natural bushland which had given so much opportunity for adventure to so many youngsters. I wondered if the people who would live in the houses planned for the site would ever hear the excited squeals of children being startled by giant spiders or the whipping tails of rapidly retreating lizards. Would they stop to take in tantalising wafts of golden wattle hanging in the evening air? Would they hear summer storm water surging through the underground pipes beneath their yards?

The land on the creek's south bank was cleared for building.

Perched on our front wall, up on our hill, I watched and listened, frustrated by a sense of personal impotence in the face of the inevitable, as the bulldozers and chainsaws went about their work.

As the 1970s gave way to the 1980s, the whole stretch of creek from the top of Creek Road to Chrysler Street was gradually diverted underground. Many of the houses along the lower side of Creek Road were purchased and cleared for new development, taking with them the wide grassy approach to the bridge that connected Creek Road to Marlene Street and its tall, spiky globes of milkweed which had fed so many hungry caterpillars. Mt Gravatt Plaza and its huge carpark has taken their place. The last of the wooden bridges to be removed was in Fairland Street. It was not necessary, being beside a road. It simply is not there anymore.

I left my family home in Mt Gravatt on January 17, 1983, to emigrate to the UK. I was 22 years old and embarking upon a journey of no return. I went out of the front yard via the opening in the grey block wall where a gate should have been, down our hill, up Creek Road, through the terminus, and on to a great life-long adventure. Along the way, I acquired UK citizenship, a husband, Harvey, six children, three by birth and three by marriage, and two lovely grandchildren, for whose benefit I have written these stories.

In place of exotic, but toxic back yards such as those I roamed as a child, I now enjoy my own English cottage garden, where I sit, barefoot in the sunshine, to brush my hair dry after it has been washed. Jasmine and climbing roses entwine themselves in the scrolls of a pair of reclaimed wrought iron gates, scrambling up the rungs to push their flowering heads into the best of the sunshine. Rainwater collects in a water butt, ready, just in case the summer rains hold back. Last year's potatoes shoot their new growth from the bottom slats of my wood paling compost heap.

As I write, sheltered within the private security of my own garden's high fences, peacefulness and a gentle calm pervade. In my world, April is painted in pastel hues. With early spring bulbs now passed over, I am surrounded all about by blue-faced flowers. From shy woodland anemone, bluebells and the finest porcelain star flowers, to ebullient grape hyacinths, and robust comfrey, there is a patch of blue in every bed. Those great opportunists – forget-me-nots and violets – have seeded themselves in every nook and cranny.

My pear and plum trees are covered with white confetti blossom and creamy-headed mayflower blooms are sweeping their long branches downwards to the ground like a prima ballerina taking a curtain call. Pink and cream camellias hang from heavy-laden boughs, and soft lemon, native primroses, self-seeded in every gap between the roses, nod away cheerily, enjoying the early spring sunshine.

April is painted in pastel hues.

The crowning glory of my olden-day garden is a grand, overarching magnolia. Its petals, tumbling pale pink and white, gently twist and twirl around me, pushed out by the tips of the tree's own translucent chartreuse leaves. Soon, we will have lilac, foxgloves, peonies, and then holly-hocks. The fragrance of lilies, honeysuckle and lavender will diffuse over the deck and climbing roses overhanging the garden path will perfume the hot summer air with wafts of sherbet sweetness. Visitors will open the gate and pause, seeking out the source of the heady scent of jasmine that hangs in the air around the top of the stone stairs.

Clematis will adorn the weathered brick walls above, and below, lily-of-the-valley will hide their delicate, fragrant bells away from sight amongst their luscious, fluted leaves. I delight in surrounding myself with flowers – too many to all be named – and all faithful friends. I moved half a world away, only to find I had brought much of my childhood world with me.

The march of progress in my home street in Mt Gravatt over the decades since I left has been astonishing. The little old weatherboard homes are being swept away, like the pioneering huts before them. New families are moving in – families who may have no roots in the area or connection with the generations who oversaw its transition from bushland to residential chic. I hope this record of my memories of Mt Gravatt from nearly 60 years ago will help to preserve a flavour of the history and spirit of my childhood home.

And now it's time to bring my story-telling to a close. God bless.

I moved half a world away, only to find I had brought much of my childhood world with me.

Chapter 9

An Old New World

This chapter is an afterthought. It is not written with children in mind, but adults – adults who now face the challenges brought about by the spread of a virulent disease across our world.

In the process of writing these memoirs, I have had a great deal of time to think, thanks to the current period of forced isolation. It began to occur to me that the way I am living at the moment has somewhat in common with how life used to be for my own mother when I was a child.

I am cooking fresh meals every day with ingredients being bought a little at a time, from trips to the shops on an almost daily basis. There are no meals out and no take-away.

Apart from food shopping, I can go no further than my own garden and I am having to find something constructive with which to fill my time.

I am concerned for my neighbours and aware of their situations, willing to help if needed.

There are many aspects of growing up in the time, the manner and place that I did that parallel the aspirations many people have today. There were also many aspects of life back then that I'm glad we don't accept anymore. When the current crisis passes and life returns to normal, what sort of normal will it be? What will life look like?

Will we have embraced a slower pace of life?

Can we redress the work-life balance, which has been completely skewed by globalization, back to that enjoyed by families in the sixties?

Is it possible that we could take the best of our yesteryears and graft them successfully into our modern world?

Could we rediscover such values as community spirit, self-sacrifice, and contentment that is not derived from rapacious consumerism?

Can we re-evaluate our own priorities in life and seek our sense of fulfilment in our relationships rather than our possessions?

Could we combine these aspirations with such things as modern technology, scientific and medical advances, equal opportunities and rights for women and protection for children etc., to build kinder, more cohesive and egalitarian communities?

Can we put processes in place that will facilitate a natural and more equitable sharing of wealth and the advancement of opportunities for the poor and marginalised?

Can we aspire to altruism on a national and global scale?

Can we value all our communities' children, not just our own, and put their safety high in our list of priorities?

Can we defend the right to remain anonymous, and resist the onward-marching advances in electronic surveillance?

Will we allow our leaders to sweep away the rights and protection of individuals we should have in law, in exchange for control of the masses?

So many questions.

Family life in the 1960s was played out in a way that many of us today would like to return to – not to return to the 60s, but to re-introduce ways of doing things that were so much healthier for ourselves and for our planet.

Our particular family, who were not atypical in the 1960s, consumed very little in the way of energy. We produced very little in the way of harmful emissions. Our water supply came from the sky. We used only electricity to cook, heat water and run the fridge. Apart from a television, a toaster and a wireless, we had virtually no other electrical appliances in our homes.

We, like most families, owned only one car, which was a fairly simple piece of mechanical equipment, easily repaired by its owner, and typically did only two trips a day – to and from a local place of work.

Work, for the vast majority of people, went from 9 am to 5 pm, was no further than a few miles away, and everybody had plenty of time to eat, sleep and socialise.

As children, we walked two miles, five days a week to school and back, carrying a bag of books when we were older. Many children walked much further.

We ate home-cooked fresh food every day which was mostly sourced locally. It was even possible to buy produce from stalls set out by the side of farmers' driveways.

The rich, red soil of the region was rightly used to grow food, not plant houses.

We ate a great variety of seasonal fruit and vegetables that grew in our own gardens and chickens could be kept for their eggs.

We composted all our vegetable peelings. There was no food waste (if you don't count over-stewed spaghetti).

Our food supply was not contaminated with growth hormones or antibiotics. Our fruit was not force-ripened, irradiated or covered with wax.

Our cereals were not genetically modified, nor our chickens chlorinated!

We had no ready-made meals available, not even pasta sauce, and therefore did not have large quantities of fat, sugar, salt or artificial additives in our food.

We could take roast chicken, egg and lettuce or ham sandwiches to school for lunch in 30 degree heat and never get food poisoning.

We did not cook with microwaves or eat food wrapped in plastic – in fact, we used virtually no plastic, and no single use plastic at all. Produce was sold loose and shopping was packed into paper bags.

Milk was delivered daily in recyclable bottles. Soft drinks came in glass bottles. We received payment for returning soft drink bottles for recycling.

We would never have paid money to buy water in plastic bottles. There were no disposable plastic bottles.

'Luxury' did not preface the label on food packaging. Very few foods came in packaging!

None of our cookware, storage containers, crockery, cutlery or glassware, serviettes or handkerchiefs were disposable. We had never heard of 'wet wipes' or disposable nappies.

Cling wrap was never seen in our home.

We did not spray our homes or our bodies with cocktails of chemicals masked by fragrance. Our clothes were washed with plain soap flakes.

Our skin and hair were soft from being washed in rainwater and we had no concerns over chemicals like chlorine and fluoride being added to our drinking water.

Our feet grew healthy – straight and strong from not wearing shoes.

The majority of our clothes were made from natural fibres and were hand-me-downs, or recut from recycled cloth from the full skirts of our auntie's cast-offs. Nothing was thrown out until it was thoroughly worn out.

We had few clothes, fewer toys, one pair of shoes (usually handed down) unless we had grown out of them, then we were happy to have none.

We weren't fashion victims. We wore much the same clothing our mothers and fathers had worn at the same age (elasticated bloomers, dresses with puffed sleeves and Peter Pan collars and shirred swimsuits for the girls, cotton dungarees and flannelette shirts for the boys, and homemade cotton romper suits for all the toddlers).

Our mother cut our hair the same way as her mother had cut hers when she was a child (although I never had a pudding bowl put on my head).

The furniture in our house was mostly second hand, passed down from relatives, or sourced from second-hand shops, upcycled, or renovated for a new lease of life. It was only upgraded for reasons of practicality – not fashion.

If we needed something, we built it out of scrap.

The motto of our home was much like that of the war – make do and mend – which is hardly surprising, as our parents both experienced the war and its deprivations as teenagers.

Most of our time was spent outdoors, either being active or doing nothing, but open to suggestions. We would walk for miles.

Children were all skinny, with knobbly bones poking out and we had no set of scales in our house. Dieting for children was unheard of and serious food allergies were very rare.

We rarely had holidays away from home, and the once or twice we did, they were never more than going to the north or south coast for a week. We never flew anywhere.

We watched no more than an hour or so of television a day, if any at all, as there was nothing to watch! Children were not targeted mercilessly as a 'consumer group' with advertising campaigns designed specifically for children's TV. That was yet to come.

We didn't ruin our eyesight or restrict the development of gross motor skills through excessive use of computer screens. Our friends were flesh and blood.

We knew the names and were on friendly terms with every person on our block and several blocks around us. We knew where all our school friends lived, for at least a mile in every direction, and often much further.

Our doors were never locked and we were never burgled. Our windows were rarely ever closed.

We didn't have to be electronically tagged to be 'safe'. The greatest threat to our safety was, without doubt, our own stupidity.

There was little personal debt, except for home loans. If a loan was needed, perhaps for a car, it was done through personal interview with the bank manager, with proof of means to make payments.

There were no credit cards and if you couldn't afford something, you didn't have it.

We had sufficient respect for authority that one teacher, unaided, could not only control, but successfully educate a class of fifty pupils with little more than chalk and a chalkboard.

In a school of over 1000 pupils, we were all known, by the principal, by name.

Our houses were not heated or cooled artificially and our immune systems must have been very robust with all the germs they had to cope with.

There were a lot of things wrong with the 1960s, (but my grandchildren would not be reading about them). There were also a lot of things about the 1960s that were right. We must let our children and grandchildren enjoy and learn from the simple things that amused and educated us, incorporating those experiences into their modern lives in this modern world.

Having completed my excursion into my memories of a former way of life, I have surprised myself at the place to which it has brought me. Maybe we can benefit from taking some time to contemplate our future by looking through the lens of the past.

Please take my stories for what they are – stories of events from my earliest childhood memories – not rigorously researched historical facts. I accept they may not always be accurate in every detail.

Maps

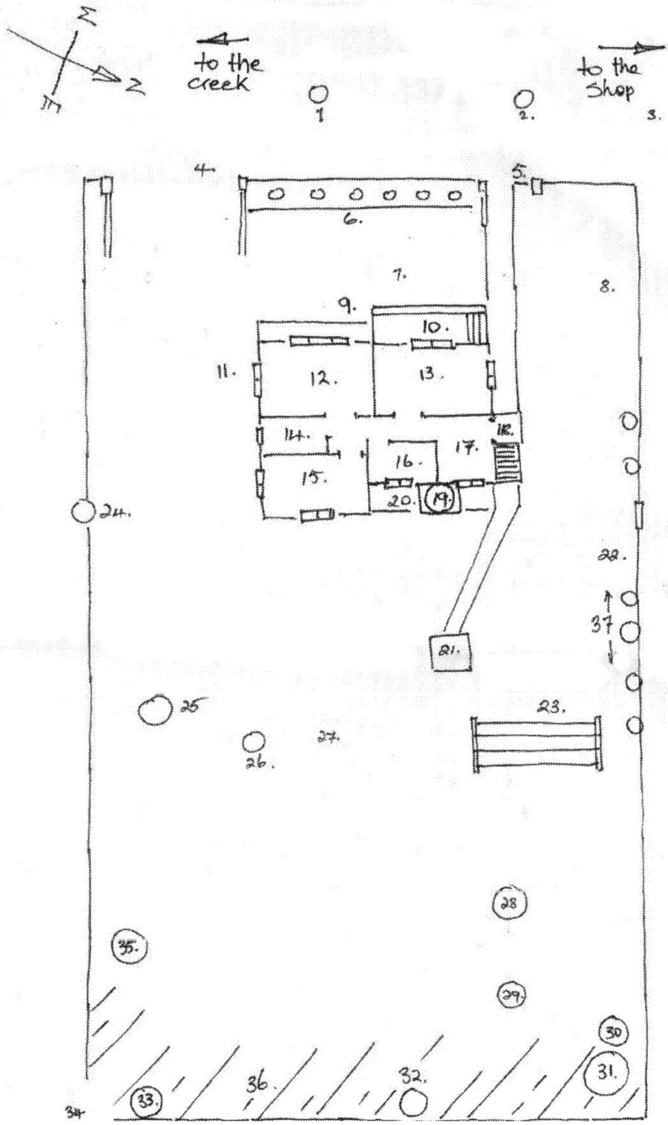

Plan of our house and yard.

Legend

1. Jacaranda tree
2. Poinciana tree
3. Autumn croci (colchicum)
4. The gravel driveway and open gates
5. Pedestrian entrance with letterbox beside it
6. Mum's rose bushes
7. Photo page 162
8. Photo page161
9. Mum's flower beds
10. Covered front porch with ranch-style railings
11. Stephanotis and paw-paws
12. Our parents' bedroom
13. Lounge room with double doors to front porch
14. Our bathroom
15. The girls' room
16. The boys' room
17. Kitchen
18. Back porch and back steps
19. Water tank on stand
20. 'On the cement' and access to 'under the house'.

Continued...

21. Old dry toilet (the ‘dunny’) with vines or shrubs
22. Side gate to Auntie Grace and Uncle Arthur’s house
23. Old ‘gibbet’ clothes line
24. Brazilian cherry tree on lichen fence
25. Willow tree
26. Lemon tree
27. Sump
28. Grapefruit tree
29. Mango tree
30. Incinerator
31. Compost heap
32. Peacock tree
33. Acacia trees
34. Hole in the fence
35. Clump of bananas
36. ‘Down the back’
37. Oleanders, hibiscus and papyrus

Mt Gravatt East

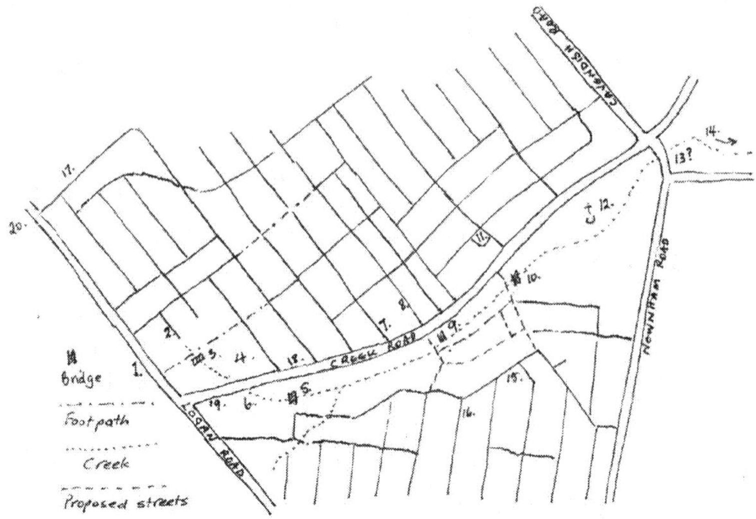

Legend

1. Tram terminus and Barry and Roberts
2. Bothwell Street and beginning of creek
3. First wooden bridge over creek
4. Site of Coles New World Shopping Centre
5. Second wooden bridge, accessed between houses on Creek Road
6. Where penny tortoises could be caught
7. Our house, our neighbours, the shop and Mrs G's house and gum tree

Continued…

8. M.E.'s house
9. Third bridge over creek where Chrysler, Dykes and Dalgety and Exchange Streets were to be developed
10. Fourth bridge and where guppies could be caught
11. Natural spring
12. Greek Orthodox Church and ten headed dragon
13. Last wooden bridge (not sure of exact location)
14. To the tannery
15. Auntie Grace's friend's house in Rothwell Street
16. Site of another pioneer shack until the 1970s
17. House in Invermore Street with pet sheep
18. Howatson's bus shelter
19. Site of photo on page 160
20. Mt Gravatt State School (Primary)

Pictures

Children walking in Creek Road, towards Logan Road in 1947. Courtesy of John Oxley Library (State Library of Queensland). The two boys on the right are carrying ports, so perhaps the group were on their way to school. The creek flows under the road from the left hand side, at the slight bend in the road, emerging into tall bulrushes on the right of the photo. The white Queenslander in the background was the house with the Macadamia nut tree on the fence next to Howatson's bus shelter. It was there until the mid 1970s, when it was demolished and a block of units was built on the plot.

The exact location where the photo was taken can be seen in the aerial photo of Creek road from 1946 (page 176).

Taken sometime in mid-1962, myself, Carol, with my older brother, Greg, and older sister, Dianne, in the front yard of our home. It was possibly the day of my christening at St Bartholemew's Anglican Church, which was about that time.

Across the road and slightly up the hill was Mrs L.'s house and her water tank on its high stand can just be seen on the back corner of her house.

The wood paling fence between our house and Auntie Grace's house, with its latched gate halfway down the fence line, was taken down not many years after this photo was taken. It was not replaced for decades, until new neighbours moved in after Auntie Grace and Uncle Arthur had both passed on.

Another brother, Terry, (with mother, Isabelle) was to join us two years later, in 1964. My much-favoured, lichen-covered fence is behind them, with Mrs. V.'s house on the other side. Past the next house down (no. 126 Creek Road and the last house to be built on our block) and over the main road was the creek and the bush.

Mum's big fuchsia bush is at the end of the flowerbed behind her, along with some giant begonias that used to make our faces screw up and our shoulders shudder when we nibbled on their acidic flowers. Other permanent residents in Mum's flowerbeds were clumps of orangey-yellow flower-spiked stems of montbretia, the bladed leaves of which can be seen overhanging the concrete retaining wall of the flowerbed.

Our father, Neville, and mother, Isabelle, with Greg, Dianne and myself, stroking Smoky (or 'Smoky-oky-oky' as Dad would call him). Taken in front of Auntie Grace and Uncle Arthur's back steps, circa 1962. A veritable Mecca of activity in the local neighbourhood, the shop's side wall can be seen on the other side of their wood paling fence.

Auntie Grace and Uncle Arthur had two grown sons who played golf and soccer (Greg is playing with one of their leather soccer balls). Sunk into the grass all over their back yard were empty tin cans which were used to practise putting. The older son, C., taught us how to hold and swing a golf club. The younger son, G., used to line us up and use us as targets for practising his ball skills. He taught us how to head a ball and shoot goals against the back of their outhouse.

My father served in the British Commonwealth Occupational Forces which were sent by the Allies to help rebuild Japan's infrastructure at the end of World War Two. He had beautiful black lacquer and mother-of-pearl inlay albums full of photos of the devastation caused by the atomic bomb which had been dropped on Hiroshima, being based at Kure, about 20 km distant.

Dad spent five years in Japan and went on to drop supplies from planes to the troops in Korea during the police action there in 1950. He may be the only soldier to have served in Korea for only one day – the day he was inadvertently left behind while doing a supply drop.

The bridge that crossed the creek at Fairland Street served for many years as a meeting place for local tribes of children. This particular version, showing signs of dereliction in this photograph from about 1975, had been a fairly robust replacement for an older, much more rickety bridge made of a few planks laid across the creek from bank to bank.

The creek could be easily accessed here from the bank to the right where a sandy path had been worn into the long grass by guppy-hunters.

Many an afternoon after school was whiled away down at the bridge, socialising, drinking Coke and smoking a sneaky cigarette. Photo with thanks to my two forever friends, R. and W.

January 17, 1983, the day I left home for my great adventure on the other side of the world. My brother, Greg, is just out of shot next to his partner, Debbie. Auntie Grace and Uncle Arthur with Bobby, their dog, are in the middle and my parents, Neville and Isabelle are at the end. The photo was taken in the front yard of our house.

I would never see my father or my godparents again and it would be another seventeen years before I returned to visit my old home and introduce my own family to their 'Nanna Isabelle', cousins, aunts and uncles.

My sister, Dianne, returned to Brisbane with her family and still lives in our family home on the steep hill coming off Creek Road, having extended it and made it very much a home of her own.

Addendum

Sometime after the publication of this little collection of stories, I came across some aerial photographs of Queensland, including the area of Mt Gravatt which I have written about in this book - photos which span the decades between 1936 and 1960.

Valuable for viewing in their entirety at: https://qimagery.information.qld.gov.au, they are now in the public domain. I have enlarged the images of the area surrounding my childhood home and reproduced them here, as it provides further information and interest about the development of what is now known as 'Mt Gravatt East' (having simply been 'Mt Gravatt' when I was a child).

In the course of studying the images, a few little mysteries presented themselves, which added to my own understanding of how our neighbourhood grew and changed over time.

The first observation I made, which caused me considerable surprise, was the complete lack of commercial activity at Mt Gravatt Central before the arrival of the tramline. I was aware that, originally, the centre of Mt Gravatt had been further towards the city centre, where the school and the Mt Gravatt Hotel are located. In fact, the two shops which straddled the junction of Logan Road and Invermore Street were still there when I was a child, before they were swallowed up by the ever-expanding Zupp's car yard in the 1970s. But I had assumed there was some reason, either commercial or residential, for the tramline to be extended the extra distance along Logan Road to its terminus nearer to Creek Road.

However, from the aerial view of Mt Gravatt Central on the following pages, which was taken in 1936, there seemed to be nothing much at Mt Gravatt Central except the odd house or two in some clearings and Creek Road itself. Beyond that, it would appear that the church building on the corner of Logan Road and Mountain Street, which would have been the Anglican St Bartholomew's, was the only community facility.

In our own street, Mrs G.'s old house, four plots above ours, is also not obvious in the photos of 1946 and 1951, but clearly visible in the one of 1960. However, there may possibly be a path that seems to lead up to her back yard and a rectangular shape amongst the trees which could be her roof. Unlike the shiny silver roofs of the surrounding properties, her roof seems always to have been dark (possibly due to rust?). The images are not detailed or clear enough to be certain.

Following on from these revelations, I was surprised to find that the streets along Creek Road didn't develop along the road in an organised manner. Eyre Street, Hawkwood Street and Gatton Street, and their connecting lanes appear to have been developed later than Hoff Street and Tarrant Street and the street grid started off more as paths through the bush than a designed layout.

It seems quite apparent, considering the order and number of houses which appeared over the years, why my parents and their neighbours had such a sense of community. There were very few of them and they were very far from any type of infrastructure such as shops, doctors or public transport, particularly before the coming of the tram. Apart from really needing to be neighbourly, they all shared a common goal – to build a home and raise their various broods of children (commonly four children per house, as ours was).

The practice of wandering across open land in the straightest path possible is evident from all the footpaths that can be seen criss-crossing through the bush and over the fields. What is not evident however, from these photos, is the steepness of the hills on which the new homes and roads were being built.

The most startling of my observations was that, although M.E.'s house seemed ancient to me as a child, it was nowhere to be found on the aerial image of 1946. There was an empty field where her house should have been.

The plot of land, which had been subsequently subdivided, on which most of the houses our block were built, was mostly cleared and seemed to belong to the house that still stands at 128 Creek Road, set back from the road. The house on the corner of Creek Road and Hoff Street (no.126) still had not appeared next to no. 128 by 1960. However, it is clearly visible behind my mother and baby brother standing in our front yard in the photo on page 162, which was taken in 1964.

By 1951, M.E.'s house had appeared behind the house two doors up from ours ('L' shaped at this time, but would be extended into a 'U' shape and become our little local convenience shop). Alongside it was another tiny house, behind Auntie Grace and Uncle Arthur's house, right up high on its block, and the house which is now there, (which I knew to be on that piece of land when I was a child), with its frontage running parallel to the road, was nowhere to be seen.

Intrigued by this new and indisputable evidence, I began to do a little further research. I came across a photograph on an historical website which showed a hut built at the back of a piece of land which housed a family while their big new house was under construction at the front of the property. I came to the conclusion (rightly or wrongly) that this may have been the story with M.E.'s house.

I had been told by M. that her husband had built the house, although it hadn't seemed credible to me, or of any particular interest or significance at the time. Now I believe, perhaps he had done so, and they had intended to live there only until the new house was built at the front of the land. The old one would then be demolished.

Most probably, due to some terribly sad circumstances, the man had abandoned his wife before the new house had been built, and M. had been left to live alone in an old shack which had been condemned by the Brisbane City Council as being unfit for habitation – probably because it had never been intended to be a permanent dwelling.

From the aerial photos following from 1951 and 1960, it appears that this is also what happened on the building plot next door to M.E. There is no sign of any building in 1946, then a small roof can be seen at the back of the block in 1951, next door to M.E.'s house. By 1960, M.E.'s house is still standing up high on her land, but the original dwelling next door has disappeared and a new, larger one has appeared with its frontage running parallel with Hawkwood Street.

My next surprise was to find that there had been not one, but two houses built on the corner of Kentish and Canterbury Streets where there is a natural spring. The area is now known as the Kentish Street Park. The houses must have proven uninhabitable, or some other misfortune befallen them in the following years, as they had been removed before the 1970s and there are still no houses there today.

What was very reassuring to see in the series of aerial photos was that things that I remember clearly, were, in fact, actually there, such as Howatson's bus shelter, with its Macadamia nut tree by its side, and the lower dirt road which ran alongside Creek Road to give access to the single line of houses that were built along its south side. Even the huge gum tree which was left by the side of Creek Road between the dirt access road and the sealed main road can be identified from the size of the shadow it cast across the field behind it on the day it was photographed in 1946.

Many of the old houses from pre-1946 can still be located on Googlemaps today, particularly those along Broadwater Road.

For those readers who enjoy poring over an old map, I have added the relevant sections following. I hope they add to the enjoyment of reading about the development of this small area of Mt Gravatt which was my childhood home.

Carol Sullivan Johnson,

25th February, 2021 and still lock-downed in the U.K.

Aerial view of Mt Gravatt taken in 1936.

The image on page 171 shows the original centre of Mt Gravatt with development along Logan Road. Mt Gravatt State School can be seen as a single building in the bottom left-hand corner with a large cleared area in front of it and a path coming up from Logan Road.

What appears to be the infamous mango trees that grew along the back fence to Herrick Street were, apparently, part of a small plantation, and the huge Moreton Bay fig tree which overshadowed the school music room is already very well established in its place. A small rectangular roof right in the lower left corner is probably connected with the site of St Agnes Catholic Church.

Opposite the school, two buildings can be seen on either side of the Invermore Street junction. Two old cottages sit beside them on Logan Road. They were very much admired by myself as a child for the decorative woodwork around their front doors, the equally decorative canopies over their side windows, and the curved corrugated iron roofs which covered their enclosed front verandahs.

When I was ten years old, a new girl arrived at our school. Her family had rented one of these old homes and to my great delight, I was invited on one occasion to visit her house to play.

Mt Gravatt Hotel faced these lovely old cottages from the school side of Logan Road, while further up Invermore Street there appears the small, square roof of a little dwelling, on a plot that faces (what is now) the junction of Invermore and Howsan Streets. I am fairly certain that this is the little fibro house, raised up on it stumps, where a pet sheep was to be found (page 11).

Proceeding further along Logan Road towards the top corner of the shot, St Bartholomew's Church appears on its corner plot and the road grid behind what was to become 'the termo' was laid out, but no houses had yet been built.

Shire Road leaves Logan Road and heads up towards Mt Gravatt Lookout, but there is also another (quite substantial) road turning up the side of Mt Gravatt from Mountain Road. This section of dirt road seems to have long since disappeared, part of it having been overbuilt by the creep of housing up into the slopes of the mountain.

An open area was eventually to be cleared which would go directly up Mt Gravatt's steep slope from Shire Road to the lookout. We always referred to it as the 'PMG' (Post Master General) track, and understood it was to facilitate the communications tower on the summit. A section of this open ground was incorporated into the cross country running course used by the students at Mt Gravatt High.

Students would leave the school grounds from the lower field and go between some houses in Suncroft Street to access a bush track which went across the mountain to meet the PMG track. It then turned back in a circular route to the opposite side of the starting point via a gap in the houses on Bentham Street.

One of our teachers at the high school in the 1970s was known to stand at his classroom windows with binoculars, scanning for groups of red t-shirt wearing boys standing around in the bush smoking cigarettes instead of completing the course. They would then wander back at the appropriate time to the finish down at the school hockey field. Such deviant children would be easily identifiable as the ones not covered in dust, grass stains and blood from multiple cuts and scrapes, and stinking to high heaven with sweat. They smelled of cigarette smoke instead! But school tales are a whole different book.

The junction of Creek Road and Logan Road can be seen in the top right-hand corner, with Creek Road going off upwards at an angle.

Mt Gravatt in 1946.

In the aerial shot on page 174, Creek Road is to be seen running from Logan Road at the top of the photo, to the junction of Creek, Newnham, Cavendish and Wecker Roads in the bottom right-hand corner. The junction of Newnham and Broadwater Roads is in the bottom left-hand corner.

The first 'street' (dirt path) coming off Creek Road is Raffles Street. Then comes Grenfell Street. Eyre Street is non-existent, and Hoff Street is only a short dirt road running up the side of the property which is now 128 Creek Road and ending at what (possibly) looks like the rectangular roof of Mrs G.'s, tucked away in the trees.

The large plot of land behind the property at 128 was subdivided into the plots on which our and our neighbours' houses would be built shortly after this photo was taken. Our house was built in 1948.

I had always believed (apparently incorrectly) that Mrs V.'s house was much older than ours, as it already had a derelict side verandah which needed to be removed. After Mrs V. passed on in about 1965, my father helped the next owners of the house to extend it at the back and in the process, they re-used the old back stairs. It was necessary to build up extra steps at the bottom using concrete, as the ground sloped away and the steps no longer reached it from the new back verandah.

Hawkwood Street would follow the line of the heavily wooded strip of land further along from 128 Creek Road. Gatton Street was straightened and roughly followed along the line of the track with a turning circle visible at the top. Many of the giant gums were still growing in the back yards of the houses which faced Gatton Street before it became the norm to subdivide the plots and sell the land with the frontage in Hawkwood Street to squeeze in more housing.

Tarrant Street, showing here as no more than a path through the bush, would become the boundary for the new housing commission area which would stretch along Creek Road to its junction with Cavendish Road.

The creek is very open at this time and paths can be seen running through the grass to crossings along its length, long before houses were built up along the dirt roads which would be laid down around it.

Creek Road in 1946 – from the site of the prospective New World shopping centre and Mt Gravatt Plaza to Gatton Street.

The location of the children photographed on Creek Road in 1947 (page 160) is at the far left of this aerial shot. The creek crosses under the road behind them, at the first slight bend in the road. The first house on the road was the old house with the Macadamia nut tree which can be seen overhanging the bus shelter right on the road. The next house along, was a rambling old Queenslander with wide, open verandahs and delicate fretwork decoration.

Creek Road must have been sealed between 1946 and 1947, as in this image, it is still a dirt road, as are all the roads leading off it. The children in the 1947 photo must have been enjoying the luxury of walking barefoot along a bitumen-covered road instead of the dusty, rutted, dirt roads, with their unavoidable sharp stones, which we still often trudged down!

Mt Gravatt in 1951.

Creek Road in 1951 – Raffles to Tarrant Streets.

This close up of Creek Road shows how housing began to develop in the closest of our neighbouring streets in the 1950s and the street grid became more established. The tram terminus was also extended to Mt Gravatt Central in 1951.

From left to right along Creek Road, we can now clearly see Raffles Street, Grenfell Street, the beginning of Eyre Street, Hoff Street, Hawkwood Street, Gatton Street and Tarrant Street, beyond which, the land for the housing commission development has been cleared. There are no Orb or Drury Lanes and Hill Park Lane doesn't yet exist between Hoff and Hawkwood Streets, although it has been laid down between Hawkwood and Gatton. Gatton Street has been straightened, and new houses plonked on top of the old dirt path.

The creek itself is still open and fairly unwooded, with paths going down to crossing points along its length. What I find quite endearing about these images is seeing so many paths, worn down to dust, by people seeking out other people.

Our house can now be seen behind 128 Creek Road, second up the hill after Mrs V.'s (with her fibro garage next to the back fence), then Auntie Grace's, then the house that would become the shop, followed by an unbuilt plot, and then Mrs G.'s. M.E.'s house and the mystery building that later disappeared are behind our row, facing Hawkwood Street.

W.'s house, where we went koala spotting (and I have since been assured that there really WAS a koala in their gum trees) is on the corner of Creek Road and Hawkwood Street and my friend R.'s house has yet to be built, joining its back corner fence to our back corner fence. Her parents spent three years, every weekend, working on their house before they married and moved into it; her mum living with her parents on Broadwater Road and her dad travelling by motorbike every weekend from Nudgee, on the other side of Brisbane. Mrs L.'s house is opposite Auntie Grace's on Hoff Street and can be seen in the background of our family photo on page 161.

My parents bought our house in 1956 and all their children were born and raised there. My mother had come down to the capital from a farm in Toogoolawah, in the Brisbane Valley at the age of 21 to work as a cashier in the very respectable department store, Trittons. She had lived in the elegant colonial suburbs of Northgate and Nundah on the north side of Brisbane. Once she told me that she was horrified to realise that my father had brought her to live on the very edge of the known world, the back of the bush, out in the sticks, the middle of nowhere. I can see her point.

Mt Gravatt 1960.

The preceding aerial image (page 181) shows the Mt Gravatt of my youth. I was born 5 months before this photo was taken and the features of the neighbourhood were much as my earliest memories of them record.

The new high school has appeared on the slopes of the mountain, with its wonderful line of giant trees running along its fence on Roblyn Street. The trees are visible as a mature avenue lining the drive of a substantial property previously on the site in the image from 1936.

Sadly, a quick view of Googlemaps reveals that they have now been removed without trace - except, that is, for the pleasant memories lodged in the recollections of countless students who waited patiently in their cool shade for classmates to make their way down the loose scree of the back entrance of the school at the end of the day. There they would meet up to walk home together, grey bags sporting the school's red and white crest slung casually over their shoulders.

The school's motto – 'Digna Petamus' has to be one of the most forgettable slogans ever chosen for an educational establishment. At least, every time I try to remember what it means, I have to look up the meaning of the Latin. It actually means: 'Seek worthy things', although our rendition of the school song had us self-identifying with the inmates of Boggo Road jail and declaring our communal ambition to break rocks all day until we died. Kids!

The primary school has been significantly enlarged, meeting the demands of the influx of families into new family homes that have sprouted up in the new roads and on great swathes of cleared bush and farmland. Every morning in the 60s, a thousand and more children would stamp their black leather shoes to attention on their rows of yellow dots on the central parade ground and shout, 'Nothing but the best!' at the tops of their voices. Lifelong allegiance to Queen and country was also declared, as laid down in the school creed.

What cannot be seen in these aerial shots of the new Mt Gravatt High are the huge cliffs of shaggy sandstone and shale which were gouged out of the steeply inclining hills as the playing fields were levelled. Built on many levels, the high school blocks were many-terraced, each terrace being held up by steep retaining walls.

The creek would soon be channelled underground to accommodate the New World shopping centre. There are still very few shops at Mt Gravatt Central at this time, although a tram can be seen at the terminus in the centre of Logan Road. The BCC and Waltons department store are yet to appear on Logan Road. Eventually, a new post office, banks and other commercial stores would be built along to the junction of Creek Road. A new municipal library would be built at the top of Creek Road in this decade.

Going to the old Post Office had been a great adventure. It was accessed via a steep internal stairwell between some shops at the central crossing on Logan Road, and could be exited on the lower ground level at the back, where several other shops were housed beneath a wooden walkway.

I would descend the stairs very carefully behind my mother with a slightly anxious feeling that I remember well, as it was quite dark, but the stairs turned just before the bottom and opened into a bright room with a counter sporting scales and various pieces of 'post office' equipment on it, including damp yellow sponges in little dishes for wetting the backs of stamps without having to resort to licking them.

My clearest memory of the other shops to be found down on this lower level is that of the bootmaker, whose shop smelt deliciously in the summer heat of leather and saddle wax and whose window was filled with work boots and leather bootlaces of various shades of tan and brown hanging in great bundles by the door. It was the first place I encountered the term 'ox-blood', referring to leather dye, and the memory has glued itself into my mind. It conjured up some rather brutal images, but was the only colour of product in the shop that I liked.

My mother and I would go to the bootmaker to have my father's shoes resoled. There was also a dry cleaning shop down on this level. Customers could return to Logan Road via a steeply sloped walkway between the shops, or go out the other way into Bothwell Street.

There was also a second-hand shop in this parade of shops, having its frontage in Selbourne Street, which was owned at one time by our new neighbours, who had moved into Mrs. V.'s house after she passed away.

The regimented boxes of the housing commission homes, with their uniform lines of white outhouses in the back yard, sheltered families that swelled the local population enormously, particularly the schools. The new roads being laid out down Fairland Street are clearly visible in this image, being already sealed with bitumen. The creek has been channelled under the new Fairland Street and the storm drains are easily spotted in the next photo, on page 185. It would be very few years before the creek was channelled back as far as Chrysler Street and the road network joined up to Broadwater Road.

The area to both sides of the creek has been left untouched and has become thickly wooded. This is contrary to my assumption as a child that it had always been so. The streets, lanes and footpaths have all been established in a grid pattern by this time, connecting the new residents to the shops, doctors, dentists, the Post Office and transport links into the city.

The arenas at the Mt Gravatt Show Grounds can be clearly seen, and land has been cleared in preparation for the building of the 'Big Top' shopping centre opposite the primary school.

Creek Road 1960.

In this enlarged section of the previous image (page 184), the lines of the creek and its tributaries can easily be followed. The storm drains taking its flow beneath the newly-laid Fairland Street can be clearly seen, as can the dirt access road which ran beside the main road to service the line of new houses which had been built on its south side.

Rothwell Street has been laid out and sealed with bitumen, but no houses built as yet, but Auntie Grace's newly arrived friend (another family of £10 Poms) would move into a new brick house soon to be built between Fairland and Amega Streets.

Two houses can be seen sitting on the last two plots of land in Canterbury Street, just before it intersects Kentish Street, above the natural spring that rose there.

The iron roof of Howatson's bus shelter shines right on the roadside between Raffles and Grenfell Streets with its nut tree by its side.

All the available building plots on our block have been filled, except for no. 126 Creek Road, on the corner of Hoff Street and Creek Road. The shop has developed its distinctive 'U' shape and its huge Moreton Bay fig tree can be seen spreading across the back yard. M.E.'s shack is still on its plot, although the shack next door has been replaced by a new house at the front of the property.

Many of these newly built houses have now gone. They were built on two plots together, and as the owners pass on, the plots are now being sold, subdivided, and two houses built in their place. The character of the area is changing beyond recognition – these small wooden family homes with generous gardens being replaced by enormous blocks of apartments and elevated homes with huge viewing balconies of steel and glass.

My own story takes up not long after this last aerial photo leaves off, with a little girl straining to peer over the top rung of a rusty wire front fence into the dusty open road beyond. Further, newer images of the area, in fact, all of Queensland, can be viewed at https://qimagery.information.qld.gov.au.

I hope you have enjoyed reading my book of memories and I would be delighted if sharing them in this way encourages you to share your childhood memories with family, friends or anybody who would enjoy listening.

Printed in Great Britain
by Amazon

68306886R00111